A VISION
WITH
WINGS

A VISION WITH WINGS

PAUL F. ROBINSON
JAMES VINCENT

MOODY PRESS

CHICAGO

PHOTO CREDITS

Mission Aviation Fellowship: 1-3, 5-7, 15
Bill Kilgore, MAF: 4
Jungle Aviation and Radio Service: 8
Moody Aviation archives: 9-13
Paul Robinson: 14
James Vincent: 16-19

ISBN: 0-8024-7174-X

3 5 7 9 10 8 6 4 2

Printed in the United States of America

Thy lovingkindness, O Lord, extends to the heavens,
Thy faithfulness reaches to the skies.

Psalm 36:5 (NASB)

Contents

Preface

My first experience with missionary aviation was with Samaritan's Purse founder Bob Pierce on the primitive island of Borneo," recalls Franklin Graham, now president of the Christian relief agency. "There I saw firsthand the crucial role of aviation in spreading the gospel to remote areas of the world. Over the years I have flown with missionary pilots across the globe. . . . Because these pilots have a 'vision with wings,' people's physical and spiritual needs are met, day after day, in some of the toughest places on earth."

When Graham was a child, his father, evangelist Billy Graham, traveled from city to village in Africa with the help of Mission Aviation Fellowship (MAF) pilots. The elder Graham found MAF planes ideal for portions of his 1960 African crusade, "Safari for Souls." Today his son finds planes equally valuable for delivering food, clothing, medical aid, and the gospel. But he has surpassed his father in one area: Franklin has an instrument rating and flies his own plane through skies cloudy or clear.

From earliest days, airplanes have helped missionaries and other evangelists reach their destinations quickly; pilots have also ferried supplies and other helpers, including doctors and nurses. Betty Greene demonstrated the airplane's time-crunching capability in 1946, her first year of flying as MAF's sole pilot. In Peru, she flew an almost straight line from an interior base to a mission outpost by going above the previously impassable Andes Mountains. Just ninety minutes after takeoff, she was unloading cargo for missionaries of Wycliffe Bible Translators (WBT). She had slashed nine and one-half days off the standard boat trip through Peru's wandering river system.

Cameron Townsend, founder of WBT, had seen the airplane's potential in the 1930s, but it wasn't until Betty came to their aid and two translators nearly drowned trying to reach a village by river raft that he was able to have WBT start its own aviation service—Jungle Aviation and Radio Service (JAARS). "Airplanes and radios don't make Bible translation easier, they make it possible," Townsend declared.

Today, JAARS pilots prove Townsend's statement true every day. For instance, a boat trip from the translation center in Peru's eastern jungles to the headwaters of the Purus River in southeastern Peru requires 2,400 roundabout miles: 375 miles north on the Ucayali River to the Amazon, then east 1,000 miles into the heart of Brazil, and finally 1,100 miles up the Purus into Peru again. For a translation team, such a trip would require months in dangerous river travel, months that could be better spent in Bible translation. Instead, a JAARS pilot can fly the missionaries to the Purus station in two and one-half hours. The plane simply flies 300 air miles, free of all ground obstacles.

But the pilots are more than glorified bus drivers. They are missionaries. MAF Pilot John Miller shares his faith with Irian Jayan nationals through English classes and with government officials during plane trips. Clif Jensen, a pilot with Association of Baptists for World Evangelism (ABWE), describes himself as "a missionary first and a pilot second." ABWE pilots train church leaders for teaching, and they preach in established congregations. Meanwhile, JAARS Pilot Ev Smith makes the message of salvation possible as he assists Bible translators in Liberia, flying them from rural villages to the Wycliffe translation center at regular intervals.

In *A Vision with Wings*, you will meet John, Clif, Ev, and several other pilots, and you will catch their mission vision. You will meet their wives, who serve as missionaries as well. You will also meet a couple of women pilots, a rare yet welcome breed of missionary pilot, according to mission aviation officials.

The first five chapters take you with active pilots on missions in Mexico, Irian Jaya, and Liberia. Along the way we will break a common stereotype: the macho, scarf-around-the-neck, nothing-will-stop-this-mission pilot. Safety is paramount to effective ministry by these pilots. For instance, Josue (Ho-sway) Balderas, program director for MAF in Oaxaca (Wa-HA-cuh), Mexico (see chapter 1), will not fly when an approaching rainstorm or strong winds at his destination leave only a slim safety margin. "No service is so important that it compromises safety," he explains. "If it's not safe, the service is not worth it." Similarly, during the notorious *harmattan* (dust storm) season in Liberia, Ev Smith will not fly when the dust drops visibility under one mile (see chapter 5).

Chapter 6 traces the early days of mission flying, describing solo flights in the 1920s and 1930s. That soon led to the first agency for sending pilots to missionary fields overseas and the unfolding of "a vision with wings." Today there are more than forty such agencies.

In chapters 7-9, the vision of a pastor-pilot leads to the founding of the first flight and maintenance school designed to train missionary pilots. Paul Robinson modestly describes himself as "a country preacher from the boonies," but he truly was a visionary as he started the department of missionary aviation training at the Moody Bible Institute. Now known simply as Moody Aviation, the flight and ground school has sent 80 percent of its graduates into missionary aviation as pilots, ground mechanics, or radio communications specialists. Franklin Graham calls Moody Aviation "the number one training facility for missionary pilots"—he received his instrument rating after certification flights at the Moody training center.

Robinson's vision has sent highly trained pilots and mechanics to mission stations around the world. Chapters 10-13 will introduce you to these student pilots and their instructors, and take you airborne in a Cessna 185 with a senior student. Along the way you will learn about airplane safety, crucial in the challenging terrain where most pilots serve. Though the airplane reduces travel times by days, in the process the pilots must navigate above jungles, mountains, hills, and valleys.

We join Clif Jensen in the steamy jungles of western Brazil in the final chapter and conclude with a look at the future of mission aviation. Today's pilot is a professional—well trained, safety conscious, and ready to help missionaries and national pastors spread the gospel. As veteran missionary Ed Maxey declares from his jungle outpost in Irian Jaya (chapter 2), "Planes and pilots are playing key roles all the time. The plane is our whole lifeline, our link to the outside world." In the following pages you will see those planes and pilots in action, bringing the gospel to the most remote points on earth.

My special thanks to representatives of MAF and JAARS who provided information and reviewed portions of several chapters, including Bill Born and Dave Jones of MAF and Butch Barkman and Hank Cook at JAARS. MAF Chief Operating Officer Ken Frizzell and President Max Meyers were particularly helpful during a visit to MAF headquarters in Redlands, California.

While at Moody Aviation, I appreciated the assistance of a very gracious staff, especially Bill Powell, Ron Royce, Reid Berry, Mary Lee McBee, and Director Ken Simmelink. Their review of several sections has assured accuracy and fairness in the report on the Moody Aviation program. Two other experts have reviewed the manuscript for accuracy: Bob Rich, the former director of Moody's maintenance training; and John Wells, an aviation historian and assistant at the Billy Graham Center archives at Wheaton College.

Finally, our thanks go to four women who willingly opened their lives and hearts: Beth Raney, who raised four children after her husband, George, died in an air crash in the Philippines; Karen Nienhuis and Cora Lou Miller, whose husbands survived major air accidents; and Carol Smith. Their stories are reminders that women continue to contribute mightily to mission aviation worldwide.

JAMES VINCENT

My appreciation to James Vincent for the way in which he, neither a pilot nor an aircraft mechanic, has grasped and communicated the technical details involved in those fields.

PAUL F. ROBINSON

1

Welcome to Oaxaca

In a remote village in the rugged state of Oaxaca (Wa-HA-cuh), two hundred miles southeast of Mexico City, men, women, and children had invited Mission Aviation Fellowship pilots to their annual fiesta. The villagers considered the pilots, who brought supplies and transported their sick, godly men. *Surely they will want to join us in honoring our patron saint*, they thought.

The pilots, led by MAF program manager Josue (Hosway) Balderas, said yes, they would come, though they had no plans to pay homage to St. James in this typical Catholic village in a very Catholic country. (An estimated 88 percent of Mexico's citizens are Catholics.)[1] Instead, the pilots would pay honor to Jesus by showing a film documentary of His life and discussing their faith in Christ with villagers and their leaders, if possible.

This opportunity was made possible when local officials asked the pilots to show the film *Jesus*, a skillfully acted film of Jesus' life based solely on the gospel of Luke. The leaders wanted a religious film at their religious fiesta, and the pilots, who had been showing the *Jesus* film throughout the region, gladly brought their screen, projectors, and speakers to the village. Christians back home had given funds for the equipment and even electrical generators to power the projectors. Campus Crusade for Christ provided the Spanish version and produced the film. The gospel of Christ comes through clearly in *Jesus*, which is now available in 170 languages and is shown by missionaries around the world.

The MAF crew of eight and their wives mingled with the people, developing friendships and hoping to present the gospel. As night approached, they began setting up the movie equipment. Meanwhile, the visiting priest was readying for his busy day. Tomorrow he would perform many weddings and infant baptisms, an annual tradition at the close of the fiesta. The village had no permanent priest or Catholic church, and leaders looked forward to this special visit. Neither the priest nor the missions team, however, knew the other would be there.

Soon the priest heard that missionaries planned to show the film. When he finally spotted the missionaries at the projector, he marched to the local authorities.

"You can't do that!" he told the officials. "If they show the film, I have to leave, and tomorrow you won't have any weddings or baptisms." His words confused the leaders. They thought both the priest and the missionaries served God and told Balderas that they wanted to see the film.

"Well, let me talk to the priest. Perhaps we can come to some agreement."

But the priest refused to talk about the film. "You can stay here if you like," he said. "But I have to leave." Eventually Balderas and his staff convinced the priest to join them and discuss the film. They met in a small hut.

"Please stay and watch the film," Balderas pleaded. "Afterward, tell me what you think of it. This film has been shown in Catholic churches in other parts of the world. It has nothing to do with Protestantism. It's strictly about the life of Christ. It's straight from the Bible."

"I know who you men are," the priest answered. "You do all these good things for the people, but later you try to convert them to Protestantism. You have other reasons for coming to the village." The priest then cited problems that MAF and another missions group, Wycliffe Bible Translators, were having with the national government.

"Let me tell you why I'm here," Balderas said. He tried to calm the priest. "You're right. My main mission is not to come and feed these people. I do love them and want them to be fed. But I really want them to know a God who loves them—a God *I* know. I want them to know Him so bad. And He wants them to know Him so bad. And I think you want them to know Him."

The priest did not reply.

"That is my true motive. I want the people to know God as I do," Balderas continued. "The reason we bring food and take their sick out is because God loves them. He demonstrates that by having us here and sharing our lives with them.

"This is the reason we're here. You can ask the villagers how many times I have preached at them."

The priest already had asked and knew that the pilots had never preached the gospel directly. Instead they had performed acts of service, saying God's love motivated them.

"I really do want you to stay. Watch the film. Let's discuss it. And the next day you can perform the weddings."

"No, I will not stay," the priest answered. "I will do nothing with you here."

It was 8:30 in the evening; darkness had fallen. Outside in the village plaza, a thousand people waited to see the film. Balderas turned to the village leaders.

"You need to decide by yourself. If you don't want to see the film, fine. If you want to see it later, that's OK. You invited us; we're here for you. Whatever you want to do is fine."

"I'm not sure if we're ignorant," one official said. "We may be. But one thing we do know. Alas de Socorro *are the only people who have ever helped us."*

The leaders went outside to meet the people. They told the audience that the priest would not stay if the film was shown. All the people still raised their hands in favor of watching the film. The officials returned to the hut. "Everyone wants to see it. Please show the film," they told Balderas.

The priest chided the officials. "You are unaware that these people come from North America and have American customs and beliefs that are not good for you. They will bring a different religion."

"I'm not sure if we're ignorant," one official said. "We may be. But one thing we do know. *Alas de Socorro* [The Wings of Help, MAF's name in Mexico] are the only people who have ever helped us. No one, not even the government, has come here to offer food or take our sick out. Only *Alas de Socorro* have come, so we want them to stay."

"I was embarrassed he said that in front of us," Josue recalls. "But at the same time I said, 'Lord, thank You that this is true. People know that we are the only ones here.

Thank You that they want to know more about You because we are here.'"

The priest walked out of the village, leaving behind the officials, townspeople, and a group of nuns who lived there. The missionaries showed the film and afterward told interested villagers what it means to believe in Christ.

"I'm unsure how many accepted Christ as their Savior, but because of the film, a small mission now exists there." A pastor each week comes to the village by plane to lead services and encourage new believers. His journey takes only thirty minutes. By land, he would need three days to reach the people. "Without an airplane, I doubt any pastor would commit to come regularly. We can bring a pastor one morning, and he can stay two full days. And we bring supplies with him."

Josue Balderas is a young missionary pilot. He is the father of two small girls, has been four years on the field, and is thirty-five years old. (Most pilots begin service at age thirty-three.)[2] Unlike most young pilots he has been quickly thrust into a leading role at the Mitla station in Oaxaca. He is program manager of all flights from Mitla, serving villages in a 120-mile radius. Like most young pilots, he has gone through challenge and growth in His walk with God during his early adult years and cares about the spiritual welfare of the nationals he serves. And like other young pilots, he considers himself a missionary who uses flight and mechanical skills.

"The Lord really challenged me to missionary work while in the Air Force," Josue says. "I didn't even know about missionary aviation." He was an aircraft mechanic and crew chief who did not have a close relationship to Christ. Though Josue was a Christian when he entered the Air Force, to Josue the military meant money, independence, and a future college education. But a couple months after being sent to Spangdhalem, Germany, Josue met two representative of The Navigators, a Christian discipleship and evangelism organization. His Navigator friends, Bible reading, and prayer slowly turned Josue from wanting money to wanting to win converts to the Lord.

The Christians in his Navigators group joined him in a series of Bible studies that fueled his passion to evangelize the lost, both in the military and eventually in Mexico, his birthplace. Later, he told his Navigator friends he wanted to be a missionary pilot. One mentioned Moody Aviation as a good school and Mission Aviation Fellowship as a major mission for pilots. Josue filed the information away and pursued the inspiring yet challenging discipleship program. Six other pilots, their Navigator leader, and Josue stayed busy memorizing Scripture, studying the Bible, and praying together.

"Through our study I developed an intense desire to return to Mexico and reach my people. What I learned was the basic stuff, but the actual living it—working out the Christian life—was something I never had done before." Now Josue and his friends from several Navigator small groups witnessed in the barracks. They formed a soccer team and grew close, winning several games in the process.

"Once I knew there were missionaries who were aviators, I became very interested. I was enjoying working with planes in the Air Force. Since the Lord gave me those skills and I enjoyed it, I got excited when I heard there was such a thing as missionary aviation." While completing his Air Force tour of duty, Balderas wrote MAF about his interest.

He returned to California after his Air Force duty and decided to prepare for becoming a missionary pilot on his own. He took courses in airframe and power plant at a community college for two years, and he enrolled in flight school to log hours for a pilot's license. But the full-time course work and a full-time job competed for his attention. Josue felt overwhelmed and decided to look at Moody Aviation. A few friends at his church recommended Moody Bible Institute in Chicago, even though they were students at Biola University, a Christian school in nearby La Mirada, California. Josue's pastor also commended MBI as strong in missions. Later some officials at MAF offered a similar endorsement for Moody's missionary aviation program. "They told me that Moody had the best aviation program."

Josue completed MBI's two-year pre-aviation program in Bible and general education in 1982, and the Moody Aviation requirements in an additional two years, thanks to his one-year training in airframe and power plants. Josue planned to return to his birthplace, Mexico, as a pilot; his wife Lynn, fluent in Spanish, would be his helper. During his senior year at Moody Aviation, Josue flew cross-country as required. The trip included a stop in Mexico. There MAF leaders told him they needed Mexican pilots and invited him to apply to the mission. The government was limiting visas and were suspicious of the program. As a Mexican national, however, Josue would not need a visa, and the government surely would not be suspicious of him.

Initially Josue was uninterested. Though he had contacted six aviation organizations, including MAF, he didn't want to live in a missionary compound, thinking he would be isolated from the Mexicans he wanted to serve. Instead, he would either go independent of a mission or join a small one where he could be part of the community. Nonetheless, after graduating from Moody Aviation, Josue decided to drive with his wife to the mission station in Mitla. He also investigated other flying opportunities in the area, but he began to reconsider MAF while visiting with the agency's new program director. Duane Marlow had the same missionary vision as Josue. Marlow wanted pilots to continue to service other missions agencies, but he also felt pilots should help to link the isolated villages to services and the gospel.

"There are hundreds of villages and we want to provide services and also promote new churches," Marlow said. MAF would do that by bringing pastors into the area to start churches and introduce the gospel to the isolated villages. But the reduced number of visas was changing the MAF work, Marlow said. Several missions agencies were unable to continue a strong ministry because of visa restrictions, and MAF was flying fewer missionaries. The agency wanted to move directly into the villages with Mexican pilots. Again, Josue could join them.

"For the first time, I became truly interested in MAF because of their expertise and the opportunity to share the gospel," Josue says. He also accompanied local pastors entering the villages. "Watching [MAF] in action confirmed my desire to be part of the local church going into remote places."

The local Mexican pastors were promoting missionary work in the churches as they took "the whole gospel into isolated regions," Josue notes. During their drive back to California, Josue told Lynn he was applying formally to MAF to be a missionary pilot in southeastern Mexico.

Two years later they arrived in Mitla, after learning several lessons in patience. Josue admits he was very independent then—he had wanted to work as a pilot alone to meet the villagers on his own instead of being part of a missions team. He had always been that way. At fifteen he left home to meet other Christians and learn English his way, in the United States. Later he resisted attending Moody Aviation, despite recommendations, choosing to go to a local college for mechanical training.

As he began to raise prayer and financial support, God taught him greater trust and dependence. The new manager of Latin America operations said, "Don't think that because you're from Mexico, you're automatically going to Mexico. Wherever MAF needs you is where we will put you." Josue had a hard time accepting that reminder that missionaries go where needs are, not where they desire.

"I went through all this [preparation], because I believe the Lord wants me back with my own people. Now in joining MAF I learn I could be anywhere in the world. That could be all right, but that is not where my desire was."

For one year Josue was unsure whether they would accept him and whether he even wanted to stay with the mission. At first Josue was confused. *Why did You lead me this far, God? They once were excited to use me. Now they aren't sure. Why?* Those thoughts did not lessen when leaders told him that the Mexico ministry itself was indefinite. They could scale back the program or end it because of political and financial obstacles. *I could go through the whole process of choosing a mission again!* Josue told himself.

Josue finally arrived in Oaxaca to fly among twenty landing strips, some of the toughest worldwide for MAF pilots.

Eventually he realized that God wanted him to stay with MAF and accept any obstacle. "Lord, You want me. I will simply be submissive," he prayed one night. "I know I must be submissive to MAF. You are truly working through MAF, and they're doing this for You, so I have to allow myself to be put in a situation where I must trust You that they will make the right decision."

Months later Josue was accepted and "it was go for Mexico," he says. All the uncertainty and turmoil were positive, Josue now concludes. "I had to admit to God 'Maybe this is my own desire. If You want me somewhere else, I'll have to trust that I will then make the right decision.'"

Josue finally arrived in Oaxaca to fly among twenty landing strips, some of the toughest worldwide for MAF pilots. "Every strip is different, of course," Josue says. "MAF classifies strips as A, B, or C, with C being the worst. We have all C strips, except at our Mitla station. So landing is a concern all the time." Often pilots in southeast Mexico face tricky crosswinds that try to push the planes off the strip. Most are one-way strips that permit pilots only one type of landing approach. And every one changes according to the weather. After a heavy tropical rainstorm, the pilots contact ground communicators to evaluate whether to take off for their destination. A soft and muddy strip will play havoc with the landing, grabbing tires and possibly turning the light aircraft. Unexpected pools of water can make braking difficult and dangerous.

Countless mountains and hills punctuate the quiet valleys and numerous meadows. The station rests at 5,600 feet, rimmed by hills, and the neighboring airstrips vary in elevation from 4,000 to 5,000 feet. The threat of landing accidents in this area is high. Josue learned how high when he arrived. Program Director Marlow told Balderas about a potentially critical accident he had had only a month earlier. A propeller broke off in flight, but somehow Marlow managed to land the plane without injury. The plane suffered slight damage in landing, but it would not fly again for months.

Equally unsettling, the Mexican government had told Marlow that his flight permit limited him to training pilots. He should not be transporting passengers, including missionaries, they ruled, and no longer could do so. That news was as distressing to Balderas as hearing about the recent accident. Accidents could be avoided, but if a flight director could no longer perform his ministry for pastors, missionaries, and local residents, the MAF program itself was threatened. Josue could receive training under Marlow, but meanwhile the program director could not perform his ministry. It appeared that no pilot could fly the missionaries, and with the government denying visa renewals, Marlow probably would have to leave.

"Here he was with me, a brand new pilot," Josue says. "If he leaves, the program closes—MAF won't leave me here by myself. It was bad news. I asked myself, *Why am I here?* As far as trusting in God, the story never ends, I guess."

For six months Josue underwent intensive field training with Marlow. The program director taught him how to fly the different strips. He explained the changing terrain and maneuvers and, of course, the politics and bureaucracies of the local governments. The director and his student had completed most of the training when Marlow left because of family needs and the government's restrictions. During their final months together, Josue learned that the government had charged the MAF governing board, located in Mexico City, with failing to pay certain fees. The missing payment, apparently lost in the paperwork, threatened to close the mission in Oaxaca. Back home, MAF leaders looked at the impasse and began to think about closing the mission.

As MAF pondered the mission's future, Josue began to appreciate his budding ministry to local villagers. They sensed his compassion for them and natural understanding of the culture. Ironically, he learned most about the value of the MAF ministry when he himself walked away from an accident. During his third landing one day, a supporting bracket on the landing gear cracked as the airplane was braking halfway down the airstrip. The plane quickly listed to the right, veering off the runway. Josue tried unsuccessfully to steer the plane back onto the strip. Instead, the right landing gear jumped a large rock and the left gear struck it.

The plane spun sharply to the left and the entire gear collapsed. The right wing quickly hit the ground. Though the engine was undamaged and the propeller had only minor damage, the crippled gear and wing left the plane useless.

The long hike made Josue understand their tough daily lives and how the pilots help.

Josue hiked for two days, up mountains and down into valleys. By nightfall of the first day, after seven hours of walking, he reached the next village. The next morning he walked six more hours over rugged terrain, down a valley, across a river, and up a hill. Finally some coworkers with a pickup truck met him.

When the men of the nearest village heard about the accident, several came to see whether Josue was OK. They wished him well. Among the group were several new believers who had received Christ as Savior when the pilots showed the *Jesus* film in their village. The new believers, though few in number, came over the hills to the MAF station to thank Josue for his part in their finding Christ.

"They made me aware of the influence we were beginning to have in those areas. There were now believers because we had gone there." In addition, the long hike made Josue understand their tough daily lives and how the pilots help. "Those hikes are an everyday part of their lives. These people are really living and dying with sickness. Things that are common in America and we can easily treat are serious problems for them—typhoid and TB, for instance. Had I not had the accident and walked out, I would not have known the reality of their tough lives."

Still, Josue was convinced MAF would not continue in Oaxaca. One plane lay damaged and Josue himself caught typhoid fever, becoming very ill. Josue realized that he was in a keen physical and spiritual battle. "Here we are with no airplane, I was sick, and things in Mexico City were not working out."

Months later MAF decided to end its role in the Oaxaca ministry. Josue, their remaining pilot, was not fully trained and was recovering from typhoid. The MAF Mexico City board had not satisfied government requirements. MAF concluded that they would reassign Balderas to another field after his recovery. The young pilot accepted their decision as correct but was still confused about God's reasons for shutting the Oaxaca program. "After all my preparation, I wondered what God was doing."

Josue, Central America director Roy Haglund, Latin America regional director David Jones, and a MAF board member flew to Mexico City and met with the governing board. They formally told the board that MAF headquarters would withdraw from the ministry. The governing board, composed of successful Christian businessmen, listened quietly. The governing board had begun twenty-five years ago and was designed to be a liaison with the Mexican government. Composed of local citizens, the board members had acquired increasing power over the years, but their incomplete reporting and part-time management had caused disputes with the government.

Neither the director nor Josue tried to change the members' minds. Instead they said thanks for the times of ministry. "You have the airplane and the building. You're the board. The equipment is yours. Thank you for this opportunity to serve you. Now we're ready to leave," Jones said simply. They were relinquishing their involvement and by law would leave the facilities and planes behind.

The MAF representatives rose to depart. What happened next Balderas calls "the first miracle."

"Well, you're right. It's time to make a change. Would you consider staying in Mexico?" one member asked the Oaxaca team.

"They wanted us to take over everything, including the planes and starting the program anew, even with new people," Balderas explains. He was stunned, considering the long-term members set in their ways. "All of a sudden, all control was given back to MAF."

MAF officials conferred about the proposal and then one official said, "We'll resume the program if all the board members resign. We will put new people in the positions to take control of the entire operation. How we conduct business and run the ministry will be at our discretion."

The board agreed. That was another miracle, according to Balderas. The chairman of the civil board also agreed to redo misplaced and incomplete paperwork. After four months, the paperwork was back in order and *Alas de Socorro* was operating again with a new civil board.

Mission Aviation Fellowship began board operation on a trial basis. Jones now turned to Balderas. "Josue, you're it. We want you to be the program manager. Do you believe we can still have a ministry that impacts the people?"

"Yes. I know we can, without a doubt," Balderas answered.

With no other pilot at Mitla and an infant board in place, Balderas began directing Oaxaca operations. Three years later he is one of three pilots flying two Cessna 185s and a Cessna 206 across the territory. Josue has upgraded airstrips, added a few new ones, and improved relations with the government.

"I'm sure Josue's preference would have been not to have had that position (program manager) so quickly," notes Latin America regional director David Jones. "Yet once MAF put him in that position, the abilities that God gave Josue blossomed. He's an example of what happens when a person rises to a need. He has good technical abilities and a good sense of safety. He wants to do things right."

> *"He wants to be their pastor,*
> *and they see his pastoral heart.*
> *That's the epitome of a missionary pilot."*

Josue also has built a network of friendships that have opened the way for both evangelism and greater cooperation with officials. "He has spent several overnights with people," Haglund says. "He finds out their needs, their aspirations and hopes. The people love him." Josue has developed a positive relationship with the key civil agency representative in Oaxaca, the commandante. One day he asked the commandante, "What can we do to get everything in perfect order for the government?" The commandante gave him a long list, and Josue did all the tasks. He straightened the paperwork and enforced the required maintenance inspections. He made sure that parts that arrived from the United States had proper receipts for customs.

"As a result, he gained the respect and admiration of the commandante," Jones says. Most program managers "develop some friendships during their contacts but concentrate on flying," according to Jones. Josue, however, "is able to make contacts and build friendships."

The three MAF pilots based at Oaxaxa transport three Wycliffe missionaries, a missionary with United Indian Missions, and several nurses, doctors, and dentists with a medical mission. They also fly pastors and members of local churches into the other villages. "We want the local churches to get the vision for what we are doing." Balderas estimates that 70 percent of the villages desire the pastors and missionaries to teach about Jesus. MAF pilots often stay with the pastors to assist in ministry.

As program manager he coordinates all flights, inspects planes to be sure they are airworthy, and acts as liaison with the government. But he yearns for the spiritual salvation of the people. Often he visits local Mexican churches to request prayer support and participation as MAF helps to evangelize nearby villages.

"There are still places in Third World countries where we are the only link to Jesus. People are hungry in Oaxaca. I'm from Mexico, yet I never knew about these isolated places where people are desperate to know about Jesus. It's exciting that God can use me to do the flying to bring the people to Him."

During a recent furlough Josue told MAF President Max Meyers, "Sometimes I feel torn down the middle. I know flying planes is my job, my task. But everywhere I go the people want me to come and be their pastor."

Meyers marvels at the motivation of his young pilot. "He wants to be their pastor, and they see his pastoral heart. That's the epitome of a missionary pilot."

Notes

1. Edythe Draper, ed., *The Almanac of the Christian World* (Wheaton, Ill.: Tyndale, 1990), p. 123.
2. Based on average starting age for an MAF pilot during the years 1989-1991; from MAF personnel records, Redlands, California.

2

View from a VFW

John Miller is a VFW—a veteran of flying wars. But he wouldn't call it a war, and in part he's right. It's a ministry. But the thick jungle foliage of central Irian Jaya, the steep hills, the unexpected emergencies, and, most of all, the spiritual struggle to bring people into God's kingdom make it seem like a war.

Though 80 percent of the Indonesian people are Muslim in varying degrees, on the east Indonesian island of Irian Jaya people are more animistic than Muslim.[1] They believe spirits are in everything and fear evil spirits much more than their fellow man. Several of the primitive tribes people are also cannibalistic. Ironically, however, animism makes the people open to the gospel. "They relate everything to spirits somehow," John notes. "They live in a spirit world in their thinking. They see spiritual warfare as a real issue. With our Western pragmatism, Americans tend to overlook it."

As a result, when tribes people become Christians, "they are more attuned to spiritual things than Westerners are," he says. John knows the people and their needs well. For nineteen years he's flown Cessna 185s and 206s, float planes, and helicopters into the villages and jungles of Irian Jaya, one of the largest of the 13,500 islands that cover 741,100 square miles of Indonesia. The veteran Mission Aviation Fellowship pilot brings the people food, water systems, medical aid, and, most of all, spiritual salvation through Jesus Christ.

John remembers the long quest to bring spiritual light to the Vakabuis village. He first flew his Hughes 500 helicopter years ago along Irian's vast South Coast in search of the tribe. Six months earlier MAF pilot Jim Harris had ferried Margaret Stringer, a missionary with The Evangelical Alliance Mission (TEAM), and two Irian Christians, Dominggus Mayor and Noak Fiak, to the village near the Brazza River. The helicopter's engine attracted tribesmen from their fields and tree houses to the landing site in front of the ceremonial house. The greeting party was suspicious: a group of naked men running out of the ceremonial longhouse, dancing wildly and chanting.

Once pilot Harris had left, they grabbed the three passengers and began dragging them to the longhouse. Miss Stringer feared that these known cannibals might have had lunch on their minds, and the missionaries resisted. But the natives pulled the strangers inside. Though comfortable with the men because of their dark skin, several villagers placed their hands on Margaret's blouse to see if she were a human female. Her blouse quickly darkened with muddy fingerprints as they touched this "white ghost" with the light skin and white top.

Stringer, a skilled linguist, began to speak in their Citak tongue and presented gifts to the village chief and others. The villagers calmed, and eventually Noak presented the gospel.[2] Later Stringer would present a New Testament to the chief, Pau, telling him they came to explain the words in the book. She left the New Testament with them as a reminder that they would return. After a meal with the villagers the three went outside to rendezvous with Harris.

Now six months later John Miller flew the three missionaries and Margaret's translation helper, Titus Fiak, back to the village. John stayed with the group instead of returning to base, and the men began to examine this strange white man. *He must be a god*, some thought. A brave warrior touched John again and again, to be sure he was human. The tribesman shouted when he soon felt John's navel. The others asked to see, not believing the pilot was human.

"It was embarrassing to me, but they sure were relieved," John recalls. "They held my arm, not knowing whether I was a spirit." After that surprise introduction, the visit proceeded well.

Months later John and Clarence Gillett, another TEAM missionary, returned with Noak and Titus. The evangelists assumed their biblical names after becoming Christians, and they welcomed the chance to tell these recently discovered villagers about Jesus for the first time. The villagers greeted the four men by jumping and chanting. They continued chanting and dancing as they half-led, half-dragged them along the logs to the ceremonial longhouse.

The welcome certainly is enthusiastic, John thought. *They seem so friendly.* "Later Margaret explained that the chanting, dancing, and holding on to us showed their fear," John says. "A mistake on our part could have killed us."

The people calmed when someone recognized John and Clarence from previous visits. Soon Noak took out a hand-cranked cassette player and began telling the creation story, using several large pictures. The voices from a cassette player and pictures were new and entrancing. *Strong magic!* they thought. Then John raised his camera and snapped a picture. At the click of the shutter, several people gasped, and hands clamped John's wrist and arms.

"*Baas! Baas!*" ("Don't! Don't") they shouted, panic on their faces. John started to rewind the film, and they yelled even more. Several ran outside in fright, while others reached to stop his hands. "*Baas!*" John quickly realized they regarded the camera as a fetish with sinister black magic power. John put his camera away, apologized, and the fearful men calmed. The evangelists resumed the Bible story.

Though the villagers did not respond after the story, they invited the national evangelists, as well as Gillett and Miller, to a noontime feast. The visitors left late that afternoon, and soon the Evangelical Alliance Mission decided to start a ministry in the village to evangelize the Vakabuis people. At one point, three TEAM women, two nurses and linguist Margaret Stringer, lived in the village.

The village was still non-Christian, though the Vakabuis' cannibalism ended in a couple of years. Though some women showed an interest in a God who loved and forgave, Pau was unmoved, and no one would receive Christ if the village chief opposed the message. It seemed unlikely that the men would leave their fetishes, rivalries, and fear for the Christian message. Though a half dozen pilots continued to fly national evangelists and missionaries in float planes and helicopters, there were no decisions for Christ. Then one day, five years after Jim Harris first brought missionaries to the remote village, Bidaw, the assistant chief, came to Stringer with questions.

"Is it true that God saw me when I ate the flesh of those men I killed?"

"Yes, that's true."

"Is it true God saw me when I kidnapped those women [from another tribe]?" he asked.

"Yes," the missionary said.

"Well, I want Him to forget it."

The tribe has no word for forgiveness, so Bidaw said simply that he wanted God to forget the deed. Bidaw had resisted the gospel those five years; now he seemed to understand and want Christ in his life.

---

*In the [Vakabuis] tribe,
twins are considered bad: one supposedly
has been fathered by an evil spirit.*

He prayed. "God, I have killed and eaten people. I split that man's chest open with an axe. I have stolen women. God, don't think about that anymore." Stringer and the other missionaries were thrilled, for Bidaw had a new life in Christ. He had confessed his sins, and, according to Stringer, his plea for God to forget was his way of asking forgiveness.

Then one day his wife gave birth to twins. In the tribe, twins are considered bad: one supposedly has been fathered by an evil spirit. Usually the tribe kills one of the newborn twins by strangulation, squeezing sticks against the throat.

"Both my children will live," Bidaw told the missionaries, "because I've trusted Christ now."

John was on furlough, representing MAF at a student missions conference, when he heard Richard Winchell, TEAM general director, tell Bidaw's conversion story. For the first time John knew the Vakabuis assistant chief was a Christian and that the rest of the tribe could become believers as well. "I was electrified," John says. Since then several men and women have received Christ as Savior.[3]

John Miller, VFW, does not always see dramatic or quick results. Yet in his flying wars he finds great satisfaction in ministry. For a nation's spiritual needs, he brings missionaries and Irian pastors into remote villages. For their physical needs, he brings food and even pipes for drinking water. With government permission, MAF pilots have flown thousands of PVC plastic pipes to villages in the past fifteen years. The people now save miles of walking to a river because the water flows through the pipes into the center of the village. Before missionaries—MAF, the Christian and Missionary Alliance, and others—flew in pipes, many villages had no running water. Having provided them with water, missionaries and local churches have the respect and ear of the people.

Some of John's flying helps local churches prosper both spiritually and economically. For instance, in Kobakma, an isolated station in central Irian Jaya, the church has its own pastor and elders. John has helped them raise money for their church by flying their produce to a city market, where it is sold. The fruits and vegetables, called *Hasil Bumi* ("Reward of the earth"), help the church meet expenses and take care of the living needs of the people.

Such ministry is tiring and frustrating at times, but ministry can be that way, John says. It's rarely glamorous but always essential. Once, before loading produce in his plane at Kobakma, he had hooked the kilogram spring scale to the plane's wing strut and began weighing the *Hasil Bumi*. Meanwhile, people on the other side of the plane were sneaking large bags of peanuts aboard that had not been weighed, wanting to get a little extra taken that trip. Such a strategy might make for a larger profit in the city, but the extra weight could cause the plane to lose control and crash during takeoff.

"Have to be a cop, act a little angry, tell them it isn't safe," John wrote his prayer and financial supporters back home. "Sweating, grunting (grumbling?), glancing at my watch. Finally I get everything loaded in the plane right up to the legal limit, tied down with cargo net and belts. Figure the bill. OK, it'll be $13. There's a fifteen minute elders' meeting—fishing in their pockets, write the receipt.

"Here's a watermelon—a gift for the pilot—given after the plane is full! Are they watching to see if the pilot will overload? I turn down the watermelon. An hour behind now, really in a hurry, still smiling, sort of."[4]

John finally climbed into the plane, fastened his seat belt, and began his pre-flight checks when the mundane became the urgent. The local pastor, up to this point absent, calmly asked John to take his two-year-old daughter to the hospital.

"She's very ill. Will you come see her and take her with you?"

"Well, I guess so. Why didn't anyone mention this before? How sick is she?" John asked.

When John reached the village center, about thirty minutes from the airstrip, he had his answer. The toddler was shivering, then hot, obviously a victim of malaria. John brought the pastor and his daughter to the airstrip and began to prepare the plane for the unexpected passengers: untie the load, remove seventy kilos, put in a seat, retie the load, refigure the freight bill. Finally the patient and her father climbed in.

"The little girl, so weak, was worth the effort," John says. Yet in his rush to unload, reload, and fly the sick girl to help, John got tired. *Did the elders conveniently "forget" to tell me about the sick girl*, he wondered, *selfishly hoping to get more produce on the plane? Please, Lord, keep me from getting upset.*

"I was an emotional basket case by this time," John recalled. "Drained of anger, too tired to cry, I just sat on the plane's tire and shook my head."[5] John got the girl and her father safely to a clinic, and the *Hasil Bumi* to market, though the distracted pilot almost took off with the spring scale still hanging from the wing.

John loves the people living in the villages spreading out from Wamena, a town of 10,000. Huge compared to the rural villages, Wamena has been home base for John and his wife Cora Lou for eight years. For four years they were at the larger Sentani base; their remaining time has been divided between Bokondini and Yaosakor on the South Coast. With four pilots flying in and out of Wamena, the station is among MAF's busiest.

"Wamena may be the largest town in the world served year round by air only."

John observes a diverse yet equally needy people in the Wamena marketplace. Primitive tribal people wearing grass skirts and other native clothing mingle with government executives clothed in business suits. The tribal people arrive with black grease across their faces and headdresses atop their brows; the executives arrive in jeeps or on motorcycles. And as the tribal crowd quietly inspects foodstuffs, city folk listen to rock music blaring from fancy sound systems.

Only two miles from this commercial crossroads the villagers live in huts with thatched roofs and have neither electricity nor running water. They raise pigs and cultivate vegetables. Meanwhile, in town a big satellite dish beams TV signals to government officials and a microwave relay station for international phone calls.

Wamena has no major roads, and all mail arrives by plane. "Wamena may be the largest town in the world served year round by air only," John says. "During certain times of the year some larger Soviet towns can be reached by Aeroflot (the Soviet national airline) only. But here we have a town of 10,000 with no roads in from the coast."[6]

Tens of thousands of villagers live outside Wamena, and, through dozens of airstrips, MAF has become a vital link to these people. MAF pilots ferry foodstuff as well as spiritual food to the villagers. In most villages, the people spend their daylight hours looking for food. They till gardens and hunt. Though few are starving, many suffer from malnutrition.

John is not an evangelist, though his faith is evident for all to see. He worships with the Indonesian people at church in Wamena and has many opportunities to express his faith in Jesus. Both John and Cora Lou have taught courses in English as a second language and in amateur radio. During the radio classes to Muslim government officials, John developed friendships that allowed him to share his faith.

"John is a quiet guy, but very deep," says Boyce Rueg-segger, program director for Irian Jaya. "He's very committed to evangelism and concerned about the service we give to everybody, missionaries and the national people alike." Paul Lay, MAF's regional director for Asia, adds, "John has a real heart for ministry. He wants to see the people be evangelized and nurtured. That desire to meet those needs he sees, whether spiritual or physical, has kept him in Irian Jaya."

John regards his mechanical skills and flying abilities as given by God to aid the church. "God gave me these talents to build the kingdom and make a difference. That gives me a great sense of satisfaction."

Meanwhile, John's mechanical and flight skills help missionaries and Irian villagers alike. Besides flying missionaries to villages in only minutes, whereas travel would take days otherwise, John does some mechanical troubleshooting. For years Ed and Shirley Maxey, missionaries with the Christian and Missionary Alliance, eked out enough electricity from their small generator to power lights for a few hours each night. But the gasoline for the generator and the kerosene to operate their refrigerator had to be flown in at great cost.

When John saw their dilemma, he read a couple of books on designing and building a simple water turbine. Then he spent a year building a cross-flow turbine to generate power. The finished turbine runner, twelve inches in diameter and eighteen inches wide, looked like a treadmill for an overgrown hamster. The second year he constructed a frame to hold the turbine runner, nozzle, and generator. Eventually John flew all the parts to the Maxeys' station for assembly. Finally, he added three large pipes that would channel water down to the turbine nozzle from the reservoir pond fifteen feet above.

Years later the turbine still runs smoothly, producing a modest 1,500 watts continuously. Ed or an associate needs only to grease the bearings each month and clear gravel from the holding pond. With twenty-four hour electricity, the Maxeys have constant power for their lights, refrigerator, freezer, and, most important, Shirley's computer as she hurries to finish her Scripture translation work.

"Do you realize what it's like, after nearly thirty years, to have electricity day and night?" Ed asks. "The pilots are lifesavers!"[7] John and other MAF pilots shuttle the Maxeys from their highland station down to their lowland jungle outpost. The pilots bring them vital equipment, mail, and medical supplies from the MAF base in Wamena. During the Maxeys' thirty years, the pilots have made dozens of emergency flights to hospitals that saved lives.

"Planes and pilots are playing key roles all the time!" Ed declares. "The plane is our whole lifeline, our link to the outside world."[8]

John put his thumb on the man's artery to stop the bleeding. Then, as the warriors and women watched in silent amazement, he placed the man in the plane and flew away.

A spiritual lifeline, however, is the most gratifying to John, who remembers a special spiritual odyssey in Langda. He ferried Jan and Jannie Louwerse, missionaries with the Netherlands Reformed Congregation, to the remote Langda airstrip. The tribes people accepted the couple, who then brought two national evangelists to help. Still, the natives were cannibals and a "fierce people," John says, and the Dutch couple kept two shotguns in their tent.

One day as he completed the landing, John saw warriors on the airstrip. The warriors had shot an arrow into a foe's leg. As the missionaries and John came out of the plane, the women gathered and began singing a death chant.

John put his thumb on the man's artery to stop the bleeding. Then, as the warriors and women watched in silent amazement, he placed the man in the plane and flew away. Doctors treated the man at the hospital, and two weeks later John returned the man to the village, nearly recovered from his wound.

"Years later, that man became an elder in their new church. Now thousands of people are Christians in this valley," John says. The villagers send people to other areas as missionaries and operate a Bible school. "Within ten years they went from the Stone Age to being a missionary-sending local church."

John has flown single-engine planes, either land or float, for most of his years in Irian Jaya, but he has also flown a helicopter four and one-half years into remote places where dense jungles or mountainous approaches make airstrips impossible. The trips generally are routine, reminding pilots that ministry is rarely glamorous. But one day's mission remains forever in John's mind as a reminder of the risks in missionary aviation—but also of God's protection.

At 8:20 A.M. John lifts off from Boma, one of the smallest of six MAF bases in Irian Jaya. The morning is normal—busy yet uneventful. Aboard are two national Bible teachers. John delivers the first teacher to Ugo, then continues on to Kawagit. Scooting over the jungle at 125 MPH, Mike Alpha Lima (the helicopter's call letters are MAL) has a slight vertical vibration, nothing unusual, and John touches down at Kawagit twelve minutes later. The second teacher steps down, and John unloads the cargo. When he is ready to lift once again, he has new companions: a policeman, a missionary nurse, and a national pastor who holds six live, yet not-too-active, chickens on his lap in the back seat. Manggelum, their next stop, is only forty miles by air rather than seventy by river. What would take a day by boat is thirteen minutes by air, and the grateful policeman gets out. In his place comes more cargo—bananas and potatoes—to join the still-cooperative chickens.

Finally, after those three stops, John heads back to Boma. He arrives there twenty-eight minutes later to discharge the two remaining passengers, potatoes, bananas, and half a dozen live chickens. Later Naftali, the Indonesian foreman at Boma, helps John inspect a fuel drum for possible water contamination. The drum's clean, so the two men pump 175 pounds of fuel aboard.

A new set of passengers climbs on: a missionary, another national teacher, and "a VIP from Holland." Less than thirty minutes later, they touch down at the remote station of Wanggemalo. John returns to Boma, loads a carpenter and his roofing material, and they head off to Uni.

In Uni the carpenter climbs down, and John helps him unload the roofing at the side of the helipad. Almost two and one-half hours have passed, and John has delivered nine passengers this morning. For only the second time today, the helicopter lifts off empty.

This engine is actually quitting! I'm going to crash!

John presses the mike switch to tell the flight follower back at Sentani his departure time and the estimated arrival time at Boma. Suddenly the engine begins to slow, and John can feel the loss of power. He hears no Engine Power Out warning horn, but the tachometer shows the engine and rotor passing steadily down through the mid-green range.

I can't believe it! I must be doing something wrong! Twist the throttle hard to full on position. No, it's already there! Maybe there's enough power to make it to a clearing.[9]

John begins a shallow left turn two hundred feet above the trees. He quickly hits his mike switch for one last radio call. His voice is steady yet urgent. "Mayday! Mike Alpha Lima is going down. One mile south of Uni."[10] The tachometer now shows the engine and rotor at the bottom of the green, moving into the red danger area. *This engine is actually quitting! I'm going to crash!*

The pilot shoves the collective down in order to decrease the blade angle and boost the RPM. The helicopter responds by entering autorotation, letting the air spiral upward to create some lift. The helicopter is in a steep glide. Near treetop level, John pulls the collective up, stopping the steady descent and letting the helicopter settle almost vertically into the trees. Rotor blades crunch into the tree tops and the crippled machine plummets to earth, knocking the pilot unconscious.

Forty-five minutes later John is standing outside the helicopter wreckage unsure of what has happened. Blood is running into his eyes and down his nose. John recalls the scene and his thoughts: "My left leg hurts like crazy, but I am able to stand on it. I realize I have just survived a terrible accident. . . . Where am I? What happened? I crawl back into the wreckage looking for my flight log."[11]

Meanwhile, missionaries across the island are praying. Many heard the Mayday call; others have been told. In Karubaga, Dani tribes people who heard begin praying and crying for John's safety.

His wife, Cora Lou, did not hear the Mayday because she was monitoring another frequency. A minute later friends told her, and an anxious, uncertain wait began.

John has survived, but no one knows.

Float plane pilot John Forsythe begins the search after hearing the Mayday call. As he flies closer to the Uni area, the beeps of the emergency locator transmitter (ELT) become stronger. Soon he spots the wreckage. He lifts the radio mike and relays a mixed message. "I see the helicopter. But from here I can't see a pilot." He scribbles a note in Indonesian, drops it into the Uni village, and turns back to Boma just seven minutes away. But it will take him and Dr. Ken Dresser, his passenger, several hours to navigate an outboard boat to the area.

Soon Uni villagers, far off in the jungle, begin shouting. John shouts back, and they begin hacking through the underbrush. Finally they break through twenty feet from John. But as they see the pilot's bloody face they fall back, crying and covering their eyes. They recover and hug him, hold his arms, and cry. Then one native hands John the paper message the airplane pilot had tossed. None of the villagers can read Indonesian, and they ask John to read it. *Heli jatuh dalam hutan. Harap tolong pilot.* "The helicopter has fallen in the jungle. Please help the pilot."[12]

They lead John to their village where he lies down to recover. The local pastor reads the Bible aloud and then prays, thanking God for sparing "their" pilot's life.

Later that afternoon Forsythe and Dresser approach Uni by outboard and are amazed and overjoyed—John is waving to them from the shore. He looks refreshed and stronger, thanks to his first aid kit and some coconut milk. "You're alive!" they exclaim, and John simply nods his head. He notices the body bag in the boat. They had been ready for the worst. A now jubilant Forsythe and the doctor string up a radio antenna and broadcast the good news. Five long and painful hours after the crash, Cora Lou hears that she really is not a widow, that their two sons still have a father.

Weeks later the MAF accident investigator concluded, "This was a fatal accident that didn't turn out to be fatal!"[13] John himself was surprised that no fire erupted at the crash site. Internal engine damage had caused the Hughes 500 to lose 80 percent power, and although the helicopter was lying upside down, the engine had continued to run for many minutes. Hot fumes scorched a nearby tree trunk. "That there was no fire is a miracle in itself. Being unconscious, I never would have survived that!" And one can't help but wonder what would have happened had the helicopter been loaded with passengers and cargo.

John's injuries were minor. He was back flying helicopters in a few months and continued to fly helicopters for almost three more years. "You know, we try to be as conscientious as humanly possible in safety, training, and maintenance—and trust the Lord for the rest," John recently told an interviewer. "I frankly never gave the accident too much thought, other than to realize the Hughes is one tough bird."

As a veteran of flying wars, John Miller trusts his planes and helicopters very much. And he trusts his God completely.

Notes

1. Edythe Draper, ed., *The Almanac of the Christian World* (Wheaton, Ill.: Tyndale, 1990), p. 114.
2. Margaret Stringer, *The Vakabuis Story*, pp. 15-17. This booklet, containing the complete story of the mission to the Vakabuis, is available through The Evangelical Alliance Mission, P.O. Box 969, Wheaton, IL 60189.
3. In February 1991, TEAM nurse Ruth Dougherty, Titus, and two other workers taught one-week Bible classes and led crafts in a Vacation Bible School format. Several children received Christ, and on Saturday five men professed Christ as their Savior. On the final day of classes, Pau became a Christian. Dougherty writes in a newsletter dated February 12, 1991: "Mr. Ondi [an assistant] reported that Pau had accepted the Lord. He had asked Pau if he really wanted to, and he said yes. Then Mr. Ondi asked if he wanted to wait. Pau said, 'No, I want to confess Him now!' Thrilling!"
4. MAF newsletter by John Miller, April 27, 1986.
5. Ibid.
6. The government only recently has begun an ambitious road-building project.
7. "The Plane Is Our Lifeline!" *Flightwatch* 2, no. 3 (March 1987), p. 2.
8. Ibid, p. 1
9. MAF newsletter, by John Miller, December 1982.
10. MAF newsletter, by Charles Bennett, February 20, 1983.
11. MAF newsletter, December 1982.
12. Ibid.
13. MAF newsletter, February 20, 1983.

3

Side by Side

B ecause of illness, Cora Lou had slept little the night before John lifted off in Mike Alpha Lima for the last time. When her husband declared a Mayday the next morning, she was monitoring another frequency. Minutes later she decided to call another missionary wife, Joy King, who had been listening to John's radio calls.

Joy had scribbled the location of the crash as the flight follower near her answered John's Mayday. "We copied you, Mike Alpha Lima." They waited several minutes for another transmission from the pilot. It never came. Joy tried to compose herself before telling the program manager the helicopter was missing. But her voice shook as she revealed that their helicopter had gone down while flying in the swamps of the South Coast. Now another transmission came. Cora Lou Miller was asking about her husband's location.

"I heard the voice of the pilot's wife come on the radio asking about the helicopter," Joy remembers. "How can you gently break the news to one of your friends, over the radio, that her husband has just crashed!"[1]

The specter of mechanical failure moves around every missionary aviator, but rigid procedures, safety training, and much prayer minimize the danger. Still, the risk creates tension for the pilot and his family. As Charles Bennett, former MAF president, notes, the possibility of an accident "is one facet of missionary life we don't like to think about. But it is in the heart and mind of every wife whenever her pilot husband is late or detained."[2]

Tired from her restless night, Cora Lou went numb when she heard the news. But within an hour her mind and emotions began racing. She felt sure the accident was fatal. "I didn't handle it well. I cried a lot," she says. "I had enough reason to believe I was a widow at that point. I wasn't sure how I would handle life and raise my children."

The Millers' sons, Joe and Ben, were both away at school when the helicopter went down. Joe, seventeen, was at a school for missionary children in the Philippines, but twelve-year-old Ben was at Sentani International School in northern Irian Jaya. A pilot in Sentani went to locate Ben and bring him to Cora Lou in Wamena.

Meanwhile his mother waited, unsure what had happened to John. She began to have regrets. John's heavy schedule as a helicopter pilot had reduced their time together. "I felt a sense of desperation. I thought maybe he had died and we hadn't had enough time together. I felt rather hopeless."

Other missionary families comforted Cora Lou, including an older missionary couple the Millers had known since arriving in Irian Jaya, Adrian and Mijo Vander Bijl. One young missionary couple, Mike and Carol Meeuwse, had been in Irian Jaya only four months. Mike began to prepare MAF's second helicopter for possible assistance. His wife, Carol, twenty-one, was a hostess that day, and her parents were visiting from the United States. "This made her and her parents realize that it could happen to them. Yet she was sensitive and helped me," Cora Lou says.

Another missionary wife and close friend, Pat Breuker, arrived with Cora Lou's son Ben and gave much comfort. When pilot John Forsythe finally radioed that John was safe, Cora Lou and the other pilots' wives cried tears of joy.

Recently John and Cora Lou returned to Sentani to start their fifth term in Irian Jaya. John now is one of four active MAF pilots who's logged more than 8,000 flight hours.[3] As chief pilot for Irian Jaya, he will oversee the safe operation of the fleet and promote accident prevention through flight training, proficiency flight reviews (check rides), and airstrip construction and improvements. Six flight instructors will help him with the training and check rides. In addition, "all of the men will help monitor conditions at the 175 strips we serve," John says.

Cora Lou does not expect John to be involved in another accident, though she knows the unexpected, including engine failures and dead stick landings, are always possible.

"I know the possibility of accidents is a reality, but I prefer not to dwell on such thoughts. The goal of MAF is not to have accidents and to develop guidelines that can eliminate pilot error. And John and I will make the best of our time together." But knowing MAF's safety procedures, she adds, "He may never have another accident."

Cora Lou says God is "definitely" in control in the lives of pilots and their families when it comes to accidents. "The risk is there, but we can do everything in our power and with the Lord's help to maintain safety."

Cora Lou is one of five wives of MAF pilots in Sentani. Of the fifteen pilots serving the six bases in Irian Jaya, all but one are married, and each will quickly agree that his wife gives emotional, spiritual, and physical comfort in their work. Together, husbands and wives serve side by side in ministry.

"A wife is an encourager," emphasizes Beth Raney, MAF manager of career counseling. Herself a pilot's wife in the Philippines in the 1960s, Beth believes the woman helps in more ways than just doing bookkeeping, corresponding with supporters, flight following, and being a hostess. The wife is also a spiritual anchor. When the pilot is "out there making very tough decisions every day as he flies," the wife can lift his spirits when "she is right in her own walk with God and can share [spiritual truths] with him. George and I would share spiritual requests as he would leave. . . . It was especially meaningful to come to the end of the day and he'd be able to tell me all that happened, and I would share with him.

"There's nothing like serving together. You're a team. In some ways serving overseas in that type of team effort either makes or breaks a marriage. If the marriage is on solid ground it is a precious time of oneness, not only in who you are as a couple but what you're doing in ministry."

"My role in just being there makes it possible for him to function," adds Cora Lou. "He's coming home at night, and I need to be there."

Pilots face stress with tight schedules, decisions about weather, and helping in life-saving situations when medical emergencies arise. The missionary wife can help her pilot-husband release that stress several ways. Cora Lou believes that the factors eliminating stress are "a closeness of husband and wife, an openness, a good prayer life, a time of sharing, and a feeling of being a team." Anticipating the end of their furlough, she adds, "John and I go back to the field with a oneness of spirit."

Cora Lou enjoys praying with John, but the busy schedules often make it "difficult to fit those times in." Her concern sounds like that of any Christian wife in the United States. "Prayer with your husband is something a wife must consciously make an effort to do, or it won't get done. Sometimes things get so busy that we can feel we don't have time to fit prayer in. Occasionally that has happened. We're human, like anyone else. Because there's always work to be done, it's easy to get caught in the trap of 'we must do this, now!' Those things can crowd out times for ourselves and God. We have to guard against that."

The busy life for a missionary wife can assume many forms.

At times Carol Smith has had to fight a busy schedule to assure daily communication with her husband, Ev. The Smiths are missionaries with JAARS, and Ev has flown two terms in Liberia and one in the Philippines. (See chapter 5 for the Smiths' story.) During their fourteen years overseas, Ev sometimes returned home as late as 7:00 P.M. Carol would serve her three children earlier those evenings, but always waited to eat with her husband. Dinnertime conversations were good, but their prayer time really joined them as a team.

"We talk openly. I can share my concerns. In praying together, we could ask the Lord to help [our mate]. That strengthens us. By praying together we realize the seriousness of the other person's heart."

She describes her husband as a "quieter personality" about his feelings. "He's more an action person, I'm more a feeling person. Everything I feel Ev knows about." During their prayer times, Ev may describe and pray for a national he delivered to a hospital. Through those words and prayers, Carol sees "the deep caring" her husband feels.

The busy life for a missionary wife can assume many forms. Like most wives, Cora Lou brings unique gifts to ministry and a willingness to learn even more. During her four terms overseas with John, she has done flight scheduling for two bases, hosted passengers and pilots at bases, performed flight following, and done some bookkeeping.

Many wives in Irian Jaya become flight followers. They chart the progress and location of pilots during the day, using two-way radios. Almost all houses have antennae, so wives can easily follow the flights. But they do it on a part-time basis, relieving the Indonesian workers who monitor much of the action. At smaller stations with only one or two families, the husband and wife are strongly linked as a team in flight following. "He flies and she keeps track of him," Cora Lou notes. "That is the wives' most complementary role to their husbands."

Cora Lou also enjoys cooking and hosting unexpected overnight guests—pilots and passengers unable to leave because of poor weather conditions. "When the weather is bad, I'm perfectly happy to put up people in the guest house and serve them a hot meal. John knows we can take care of guests."

To the mission community, Cora Lou brings two other special skills: piano teaching and hairdressing. A licensed cosmetologist, she enjoys cutting hair and giving perms for the missionary wives visiting Sentani. "It gives me an opportunity to learn about their ministry, share in their joys and frustrations, and offer a word of encouragement or prayer."

She also enjoys playing and teaching the piano. With a diploma in sacred music, Cora Lou has performed recitals and played at banquets in the island's interior. At Sentani along the Irian coast, she plays at services and accompanies soloists at English-speaking churches. She also teaches piano at Sentani International School for missionary children, giving lessons to students in elementary through high school grades.

Many wives, trained at Bible colleges, also teach. Beth Raney taught with her husband, and that ministry together strengthened their relationship. "George and I co-taught a Sunday afternoon college class and children's Bible clubs. It was exciting to be able to share the story of God's love to those who had never heard."

"I think even for safety reasons it is crucial that the man and wife have a good relationship," Beth adds. She remembers the warning of the late Pastor Alan Redpath: "Keep short accounts."

"That's true not only with God but with one another," Beth says. "That is really important. We do talk about those things at MAF headquarters before we send people to the field. The importance of the marriage relationship has broad implications and consequences in overseas MAF ministry. . . . Our pilots often are flying into inhospitable terrain and treacherous weather, and they have to make judgment calls continually. For them to have the freedom to make those decisions without the baggage of misunderstanding between man and wife is important. It's certainly one facet of safety."

Beth counsels MAF couples from personal experience. She became a widow in 1968, when George, on his final flight of the day, lost engine power after he dropped food and mail to New Tribes Mission personnel at Tabon, on the rugged Philippine island of Palawan. The plane descended steadily, crashing into a grove of coconut trees, killing George and a missionary with Association of Baptists for World Evangelism. On December 23, one day later, MAF headquarters received Beth's cable: "George's life now complete. His only desire was to glorify the Lord. Though our loss cannot be measured, the Lord has given peace. Isaiah 43:1-2; 44:3."[4] Beth has raised four children alone. Her two sons, Paul and Jonathan, are now themselves missionary pilots; her daughters, Miriam and Rebekah, assist their missionary husbands in ministry.

Intimacy and creativity are essential for dealing with the cultural adjustments.

Beth says stress on the field is a given. At MAF and other missions agencies, outgoing missionaries attend orientation school and learn about ways to handle those pressures. Surprisingly, the pressure is not only a male issue. The missionary pilot will face major adjustments to the culture, including learning a new language and customs, as well as pressures from government officials, missionaries, and nationals all asking for his expertise and time. His wife, however, has a different set of demands. "Her whole world is changed," Beth declares. "A pilot hops immediately into his normal framework of life, flying a plane. . . . As soon as language school is finished, he's out everyday doing what he knows, and what he's done for many years. His wife faces a different world. She shops in a place where she has to use a different language. She buys different foods and has to find the names for spices.

"For the first time in her life she may have to interact with a helper in the home at least part time so that she can have time to do mission work. She may end up teaching her children, doing bookkeeping, shopping for missionaries, all for the first time. She also may have many people in her home, especially if she is the only pilot wife in the area

. . . so she manages a guest house. All of this change in her lifestyle demands an immediate adjustment."

Such an environment makes intimacy and creativity between the missionary couple more likely. In fact, intimacy and creativity are essential for dealing with the cultural adjustments, says Karen Nienhuis, a missionary wife who also served in Irian Jaya with her husband, Dave, in the 1980s. (For a look at Dave's missions career and Karen's new role since their return to America, see the next chapter.) Thousands of miles from their extended family—parents, brothers and sisters, nieces and nephews—the missionary couple depend on each other more, according to Karen, and they spend more time with each other. "Dave and I became close friends. We developed interests together because we spent time together. If he liked to jog, then I would too. Over there, you *have* to be close friends."

Similarly she learned to be creative, because she had to. "A wife can't go out and buy a steak to throw on the grill. You have to be creative at mealtime." Carol Smith agrees. In Monrovia, the Liberian capital, markets sometimes run out of foodstuffs. When her family wanted a cake, including frosting, Carol didn't panic when she found the stores out of powdered sugar. This had happened before, and she had a recipe for frosting that used granulated sugar that had worked well. Now, though, she decided to try something different. Every two weeks she met regularly with missionary and support-staff wives to swap recipes and reveal secrets. Perhaps there, or somewhere else (Carol's not sure), she learned to turn granules into powder.

"You can put granulated sugar into a blender and powder it. We did that. We powdered it down and tried making our own frosting. It's not quite like U.S. powdered sugar, but it produced something that worked fine," she says. Another time she unraveled the seam from the toe of new men's white socks and began making knee socks for her six-year-old daughter. "They were great, and only we knew [the source]," she says.

For Karen Nienhuis, the greatest challenge in creativity came in maintaining her spiritual zeal. The missionary cannot attend a weekend retreat or a couple's seminar, like friends back at their home church in America. Without those spiritual resources, Karen says, "You have to be very creative. But the Lord filled the gaps, if we were sensitive to what He was doing in our lives. He knew we didn't have those spiritual resources. If we were reading His Word and were committed to being obedient to Him, He filled those gaps."

Notes

1. MAF newsletter, by Charles Bennett, February 20, 1983.
2. Ibid.
3. "Milestones in Safety," *LifeLink* (Winter 1991), p. 13.
4. Press release from MAF, December 23, 1968.

4

A Steadfast Love

M om, I have a problem." Four-year-old Karen Riley looked up at her mother, asking for help.

"Oh? What is it?"

"I can't decide whether to be a missionary or a nurse."

"Well, you can be both," her mother replied.

For several years that solved a little girl's problem. As a young Christian, Karen naturally wanted to help people. Later, however, she ran from missions service, feeling she would be out of style and ridiculed.

"I kind of stuffed it," she says, recalling her junior high years. "I wouldn't think about missions. I thought if I ignored it, maybe it would go away." Missions seemed "scary—there was the unknown." And Karen thought most missionary children were strange. "I didn't want to be out of it. The kids dressed funny and didn't know about American culture."

During high school Karen began to understand the joy and satisfaction of obeying God. She stopped running and began to consider missions. Eventually, a romance blossomed with Dave Nienhuis of Hart, Michigan, who was heading to Moody Bible Institute in hopes of becoming a missionary pilot. Dave was accepted at Moody Aviation, they married, and later she assisted him in Irian Jaya for eighteen months. She was a missionary, hosting guests on the air base, doing flight following, and most of all, supporting her husband's ministry with prayer and emotional and physical encouragement.

Karen Nienhuis, like most wives of missionary pilots, sees her ministry first and foremost to her God, and second to her husband. Ironically, years later God has lifted her from her missionary perch and brought her into nursing. She is completing nurses' training to help Dave, who can work only part-time after a plane crash caused major brain injury. Though the near-fatal accident wrenched her husband from his plane and from missions service, Karen still serves God as she waits on her husband's long, slow recovery. Dave's reasoning level is that of a fourteen-year-old, and he has limited decision-making ability. Yet Karen's love of her God and her husband remains steadfast.

"Karen has made a remarkable transformation. God has given her the unusual ability to maintain respect for her husband," says Jack Walker, a family friend and MAF pilot and administrator for more than twenty-five years. As executive director of development and funding, he lived with the Nienhuises one week while visiting churches and supporters in Grand Rapids. "Karen [knows] that Jesus Christ has made the difference in filling that void," Walker says, "and has allowed her not only to do it in the role of a wife but also as a mother, to portray Dave as their [sons'] father even though he is severely limited and cannot function as a normal father does."

"Dave's level is that of a thirteen- or fourteen-year-old," Walker says. "It would be easy for many good Christian women to find themselves talking down or actually treating him as a . . . fourteen-year-old and not as her husband, her friend, her lover, and the man she married and respects."

Karen denies she is a heroine or a pillar of spiritual strength. She says she still wrestles to accept God's plans for her. For instance, when she finished a course recently on caring for the elderly at nursing school, she hesitated about the possibility of becoming a geriatrics nurse. "A lot of my friends said, 'I wouldn't do that.' It won't be my first choice, either. But I don't want to say about anything 'I will never do that.' I believe every Christian has to deal with missions and God's plans for their lives that way. You have to give, be willing to go where He wants you. Even be willing to not go."

Karen's devotion to God traces back to the mid-seventies, when she became active in the high school program at First Baptist Church in Hart. She attended the youth Bible study every Tuesday night. After work during one pleasant Michigan summer, the sixteen-year-old and several of her Christian friends would pedal their bikes from her small town of Mears for the short ride to Silver Lake, just east of Lake Michigan, often talking and drinking malts as they biked. Occasionally there were boat rides on a friend's sailboat, and the group at times swelled to fifteen guys and girls. Sometimes Dave Nienhuis, a nice guy who visited her church often, would join them. He sang in the choir and attended Sunday school at his own church in New Era, but he visited First Baptist regularly Sunday evenings, where his older brother was youth pastor and more teens gathered than at his small church.

Near summer's end, just two weeks before Dave would be accepted as a student at Moody Bible Institute, he asked Karen on a date. The high school Bible study led by Dave's brother had just ended. Dave, shy around girls, was in friendly surroundings at his brother's apartment, and the timing seemed right. A surprised Karen said yes. He took her to a local movie and they had a fun time, but Karen was in awe. "He was 18, two years older than me, and to me that seemed a big difference in age. I was overwhelmed that this older guy who I respected and liked a lot would ask. When we said good-bye, I thought, 'Well, that's the end of that. This will never develop. It would be wonderful, but it's not going to work out."

Dave left feeling very impressed with Karen. But he was afraid she would not say yes to a second date and became so nervous that he couldn't work well for four days. His stomach was in knots, and he was unable to fill the orders at his dad's auto parts store as quickly and as accurately as he had all summer.

His father did not know Dave's ailment, but he recognized a poor worker, and after two days he pulled his son aside.

"Dave, you shape up or get out of here. Just go home. You're so moody that I can't stand it!" Dave said nothing and walked quietly to the door.

That night his dad could not get Dave to talk. John Nienhuis turned to his younger son, Bob, who was in Karen's class at school. "What's wrong with Dave?" the father asked.

"Oh, don't you know? He's in love," Bob answered.

A couple days later Bob decided to help his love-sick brother. He approached Karen at church. "If my brother asked you out, would you go out with him?"

"Well, yes. But, Bob, don't say anything," Karen whispered, hoping no one could hear them. "Don't mess with it by saying anything."

Bob, however, did say something. That afternoon he told Dave that Karen would like to be with him again. So Dave gathered his courage and asked her out.

"After that, we dated forever," Karen says simply.

They had known each other since Karen was eleven years old. "I knew Dave loved the Lord a lot, and we were good friends."

Dave received notification of acceptance by Moody Bible Institute just days before classes began, and it marked an important change in his relationship with his father and girlfriend. He left the store and a spot in the family business for Moody, "so I could work for the Lord as a missionary."

Three hundred miles soon separated the Moody freshman from his girlfriend, but weekly letters deepened their interest and appreciation for each other. Every two weeks Dave called for ten-minute chats that sometimes went longer. By Thanksgiving, they felt a commitment to each other, even though Dave had not proposed marriage. The following year, Karen visited Dave at MBI a couple times as she completed her final year of high school.

The next June they were engaged. Three months later they went to Moody Aviation flight camp, where Dave completed a battery of tests and interviews, and Moody officials observed Dave's interactions with others there. The couple decided they would set a wedding date if Dave was accepted into Moody Aviation at the end of flight camp.

The women and men boarded separately in a camp-like atmosphere, and Karen watched as many wives waited uneasily. "The school, the location—it was everything the women wanted. They were in a tremendous state of anxiety. Dave and I were cool. We wanted to be accepted, but we were at ease, thinking, 'If the Lord wants us in this, He will get us through. If He doesn't, that's fine.'"

On Friday, the last day of camp, every candidate received his letter indicating acceptance or rejection by the school. More than half would not be accepted into the limited number of openings. Dave opened his letter, ready to be turned down. Instead, he smiled and showed it to Karen.

Dave opened his letter, ready to be turned down. Instead, he smiled and showed it to Karen.

"We were really excited. Here was one more step toward being missionaries." On their way home to Michigan, they set their wedding date for November.

Before entering Moody Aviation, though, Dave continued his degree studies at Muskegon Community College while working a year with his dad, and Karen attended Grand Rapids Baptist College. At age twenty-three, the minimum age for student pilots, Dave entered Moody Aviation.

Dave had first thought about becoming a missionary pilot during a missions conference at Karen's church. Terry Bowers, a pilot with Association of Baptists for World Evangelization, spoke about his ministry and the need for prayers. Dave, who was thinking missions and loved mechanical things, began thinking aircraft and missionary aviation. As he looked through Bible college catalogs much later, he noticed Moody's mission aviation program. He knew about the school's reputation, liked the Chicago location, and especially liked the cost.

"I investigated other aviation programs, but the cost attracted me. At Moody I didn't have to pay for my education. I paid for the food I ate, but there was no tuition. My first two years at the Chicago campus I kept my bills low."

His parents paid for his lodging. In Tennessee Dave and Karen arrived with their savings, and he was able to sustain himself in the two-year program. Dave graduated from Moody Aviation with only $30 in the Nienhuis checking account but debt free.

After graduation, Dave investigated five mission agencies but kept coming back to Mission Aviation Fellowship, whose headquarters he had first visited during his senior cross country trip, when the student pilots touched down at MAF headquarters in Redlands, California. Eventually the Nienhuises attended MAF candidate school, liked what they saw, and began to gather prayer and financial supporters. Within two years they had raised support and headed for Irian Jaya with their two sons, Michael, age five, and their three-year-old, Gary.

For nine months they learned the Indonesian language on the island of Java, and then Dave began flying from Sentani, MAF's main base in Irian Jaya. He developed flying proficiency there and passed several flying exams before being assigned to Wamena, a more difficult airstrip. The main strip on the island, Wamena's single paved runway sat in a large valley at 5,000 feet, with nearby mountains reaching to 10,000 feet.

Dave brought the injured and sick, as well as many pregnant women, to the Wamena medical clinic. The national doctors at the fifty-bed government hospital let William Vriend, a skilled surgeon and medical missionary from the Netherlands, perform the major operations. Dave also delivered lots of rice, building supplies, and animals to villages, where churches and missionaries presented the gospel. Sometimes he brought live pigs and chickens to missionaries whose lack of electricity meant no refrigerators to store meats. He also ferried hundreds of eggs and "handled those with extra care," Dave says, laughing.

One early April morning after spending a year at the Wamena base, Dave took off in his Cessna 206 with three Indonesian workers aboard. Before departure, he had checked the plane and made sure the passengers were buckled in. Sixty feet above the ground and climbing, the engine faltered; the craft turned earthward.

From her home near the airfield, Karen heard a plane engine sputter and then quit. Seconds later the base radio crackled: "There's been a crash. It really looks bad." Karen had not heard the transmission, but she sensed Dave was in danger, even though she was unaware he was hurt.

She spotted Gary, now five, and knelt before him. "Son, Daddy might have just gone to heaven to be with Jesus."[1]

---

*David had two broken hips,
one crushed into more than thirty pieces,
and an abdominal-intestinal injury.*

The three Irian passengers had only minor injuries, the worst being a broken leg. But Dave was found unconscious in the plane. Somehow the plane had plummeted into the backyard of a national doctor, one of three miracles that encouraged Karen greatly in the first uncertain days of a life-threatening injury. An ambulance was near the house, and, before medical personnel even moved Dave to the ambulance, Dr. Vriend, the Nienhuis's associate, arrived—another miracle. Only fifteen minutes had passed, and the Dutch doctor quickly noticed the swelling of the head and neck. He suspected brain injury, and multiple fractures also were likely. Later in the Wamena clinic, Dr. Vriend performed the first of two brain surgeries to drain fluids and relieve pressure. Dave's breathing stabilized, but he needed better facilities for subsequent operations.

Five days later an air ambulance arrived to fly Dave to Australia, but only after a puzzling delay in Australia when the pilot of the medical jet could not start the engine. A total electrical failure forced the pilot to leave the aircraft and wait for mechanics to arrive for repairs. About one hour later, before the mechanics began work, the pilot tried the engine once again. This time the engine started immediately. Karen and other MAF personnel knew this was a miracle, for poor weather had engulfed the Wamena landing strip and an on-time pilot would have been forced to turn back, wasting even more precious hours. Instead, the skies had cleared only minutes before the delayed flight arrived.

With modern X-ray equipment, the Australian doctors determined that David had two broken hips, one crushed into more than thirty pieces, and an abdominal-intestinal injury. More serious than both, however, was the severe damage to his brain.

A team of doctors performed several brain operations, and Dave came out of a coma. Two months after the accident he returned to Grand Rapids, where he made steady improvement. At Blodgett Hospital his speech slowly returned, and he began to strengthen his right side, which had been weakened so much that Dave soon became left-handed.

Two years of intensive rehabilitation followed, including nine months at the Center for Neural Skills in Bakersfield in central California. There he received speech therapy and physical, recreational, and occupational therapy. Among the specialists was an ophthalmologist trained to help head-injury patients. He fitted Dave with new prescription eyeglasses. Dave also received much counseling.

For two years Dave could not remember the accident. Though he recognized his wife as soon as he came out of the coma, he could not recognize his parents for two months. He still is unable to remember exactly when he married Karen or when he became a Christian, but he is sure of both.

He now works at two part-time jobs—one at Steel Case, the largest U.S. manufacturer of office furniture. There Dave quickly affixes labels on two-by-three-foot fabric samples, matching the labels to the appropriate fabric. After four hours at Steel Case, a van from Hope Rehabilitation Center takes him to East Grand Rapids Middle School. At the school library Dave checks out books to students two hours each day.

"They consider me a good worker. They always give me the new job first. They watch what my time will be so they can tell what it will be for the other guys." Dave's soft voice sounds hoarse, yet it is firm and even. His vocabulary is simple; his sentences complete but short.

He now can move around at home and work with minimal assistance. At times his aluminum cane becomes a welcome third leg. He moves slowly and steadily around their four-bedroom house, and can shop with Karen ten minutes without tiring. For longer walks, they pack Dave's wheelchair in the car trunk wherever they go. In summers, Dave joins Karen and the boys at his father's home, where his motorized scooter lets him accompany Karen and his parents on daily strolls among John Nienhuis's cherry orchards.

Because of the brain injury, Dave acts differently, and Karen loves a different man. Dave has "a lot of trouble expressing emotion" now, Karen says. "Because of his injury he has trouble . . . concentrating on anything but his world. It takes so much effort for him to do the simple things of everyday life. That's very hard for me."

Although Karen admits struggling at times with commitment, her love does not waver. "I have never considered walking out. I know that the hand of the Lord is in this situation. He knows about this change in Dave. This does not alter my marriage vows. I also know the Lord is doing things in my life that I couldn't have done if this had not happened. For example, reliance on God. I relied on Dave a lot. Now I pretty much walk alone. I have good family and friends, yet day to day I am a single parent in many respects. That's tough."

The changes in Dave's life remind her that God does and should control her life. "When I began learning about head injuries, I realized this is something I can't control. I can never make our lives normal again. I had always thought if I worked hard enough and hung in there long enough I could control things. But no matter what I do, this is something I could not prevent. This situation, I realized, was totally in His hands, and the only way I could get through was to depend on Him."

Her steadfast love for Dave matches her devotion to God—not that she did not struggle with the death of her missionary vision. Immediately after the accident she began to wonder about God's timing and the justice of the crash. *Oh, if this had happened after two terms,*[2] *I could handle this, Lord,* she thought.

"We spent ten years preparing, and I thought with two terms, we'd almost have ten years on the field," Karen explained during an interview in her Grand Rapids home. With Dave listening at the dining room table, she recounted her adjustment to life away from missions. "But then I began to realize the truth: God doesn't think in human terms. Ten years of training and who cares how many months on the field—that doesn't mean anything to Him. What matters is what He wants from me. What matters is our attitudes, our commitments, and our priorities."

For the first six months after the 1985 accident, Dave's recovery was in doubt. But as he gained strength Karen began to recognize that the injury would have lasting effects on their lives. "I began to slowly deal with [our never being overseas missionaries again]. For three years, my heart ached over the loss of the ministry. Now I'm in the nursing program and far enough beyond the accident that it isn't hard now.

"I never was angry with God. I was open to His working. . . . I knew He didn't make mistakes. I knew this was for our good. No matter how hard things were, He never let us down.

"When the accident occurred, God was with Dave. He could have spared Dave. He could have had Dave have minor injuries—or He could have let Dave die. If God needed an opportunity, He certainly had it. Dave was very critical for two months. He could have died easily at any time. He can take us any time He wants. Dave didn't need to be in critical condition for God to do that."

"I still don't know God's purpose
fully in this accident."

Karen admits she did not readily trust God initially. Instead she thought, *We got through hard times before. We will get through this. Yes, this will take time but eventually everything will be OK.* But she found that the critical months of Dave's uncertain recovery made her emotionally numb. Nine months passed before Dave strengthened noticeably and Karen's emotions began to thaw. Now fears swept over her newly active mind. *Now what? We can't go back to the ministry. None of our dreams will be fulfilled.*

"Those were really hard times," Karen says today.

"There was confusion and I wondered 'Where will the strength come from? I have nothing left.'

"That's a good position to be in, " Karen recalls. "At that point, I'm through. Everything in me is gone. I have nothing left to give. So I had to scrape myself up and say, 'Lord, I know You are there. I know You will get us through this. You love us.'

"I still don't know God's purpose fully in this accident. I can see growth in my own life. I'm really a different person spiritually. And my role is different. Dave always drove every place. I could barely drive. Now I can find my way around Grand Rapids like a breeze. I've driven in busy Los Angeles and Chicago."

Karen has struggled with managing money and with role reversals. She bought their house and a car upon their return to America. Dave is unable to initiate plans or think through decisions. "Dave ran the show before the accident, and now I do it. I'm a stronger person for it, and I've learned a lot about giving through this. . . . I've learned you can be committed to somebody and love somebody even though he is not able to return that love. Definitely I'm in process."

"Before the accident Dave was a very bright individual, very keen in finances, accounting, and bookkeeping," notes their friend Jack Walker. "Karen has adjusted to balancing and making all the financial decisions, not just the big ones on housing and car. She has done it remarkably well. In the process, she continues to struggle with her own self-image. . . . She's made progress and has done things she would have never done if not for the accident. At the same time, she does not consider herself astute in financial matters. She can turn to family and friends, but she's still going through the process of [feeling] good, not guilty, about her roles."

Six years have passed since Dave's near-fatal accident. Walker visited almost five years after the accident and observed a family united by a mother's strong spiritual tie. Karen maintains "her own private devotion time, leading the boys during their prayers in the morning . . . before going to school, of making sure as much as possible they were a functioning family in the local church, getting them involved in sporting activities that their dad would normally do. All that comes from a strength that comes from a daily time of meditation, reflection, prayer and commitment."

Dave has turned his walking cane
and his wheelchair into tools for
witnessing to the goodness of God.

Often she must be the family disciplinarian. "There are many gaps in our family rules and our family situation. But God knows about those. He gives me the wisdom, the extra strength and patience I need."

Meanwhile, her husband's strong faith and courage give her strength. "His love of the Lord has never left him. From the time he could pick up something to read, he'd pick up his Bible," Karen says. "The husband of one of my friends is head injured, and he has written off the Lord. He said, 'If God is so good, why would he let this happen?' Dave never did. That's amazing. Dave could forget everything else and yet still have the love of the Lord in his heart."

Karen knows Dave has turned his walking cane and his wheelchair into tools for witnessing to the goodness of God. In no place is that clearer than at work. Dave has become a loving, yet direct, evangelist at Steel Case.

"Someone sees my cane and asks, 'What happened to you?' I tell them, 'Well, I was a missionary pilot, and I was critically injured. I couldn't get around and talk like I do now. The Lord got me through.'"

At times Dave's witness at work is powerful and inspiring to Karen. Once when a coworker learned that Dave's limp came from an airplane accident as a missionary pilot, the incredulous employee asked Dave directly, "You flew an airplane? For missionaries?"

Dave explained how he helped villagers receive medical treatment at distant hospitals and how he brought missionaries to small villages so the people could hear about God's love in sending Jesus. Then he mentioned the crash.

"I'm handicapped, but I still have the Lord in me," Dave told his coworker. "I have a great day to look forward to when I won't need my cane any longer."

"When won't you need your cane?" his friend asked.

"When I go to heaven."

"What's heaven?" he asked.

His friend listened quietly as Dave presented the gospel. Occasionally a person listening to Dave's testimony will challenge God's goodness.

Dave remembers one man at work asking, "Well, what's good about that cane?"

Dave replied simply, "With the cane I can trust the Lord to get me through instead of me to get me through."

For Karen and Dave Nienhuis, their steadfast love of God and for each other carries them through each day. The former pilot and his wife enjoy a new and exciting mission field in Grand Rapids, Michigan.

Notes

1. "Faith Helps Keep Family Strong in Face of Tragedy," *Muskegon Chronicle*, by Caryn Johnson, n.d., 1985. The account of the Cessna 206 crash comes from this news story and another in the Fremont, Mich., *Times Indicator* ("Brother of Area Minister Injured in Jungle Crash," by Maggie Hostetler, June 19, 1985, p. 1).

2. Eight years. Each term, MAF missionaries serve forty-two months overseas, followed by a six-month furlough.

5

Liberty in Liberia

Warm, humid air from the nearby swamp rolls through the house of Evan and Carol Smith at about 10:00 P.M. The two missionaries with Jungle Aviation and Radio Service choose to abandon their warm, sticky foam mattresses for the two lawn chairs. Though their children have found coolness and sleep on the floor, Ev and Carol sit uncomfortably in sluggish conversation, waiting for the electricity to return and revive the bedroom air conditioner and their steaming bodies.

It's another April night in their section of Monrovia, Liberia. The Liberian Electricity Corporation is playing "Power Rotation" again, trying to ration electricity and pleasing no one. Across the swamp, JAARS's other pilot in this African hotland is sleeping soundly with his wife and children. His air conditioner hums calmly. But for Roger Krenzin, his hour of torment awaits. Meanwhile, Evan tries to ignore his sauna, which will continue until 1:00 A.M.

"The [Krenzins' electricity] went off at one and ours came on at one," Evan recalls. "I didn't sleep until one; then I slept till seven. Roger slept from 8:00 P.M. to 1:00 A.M.; then he was restless the rest of the night."

Heat, thunderstorms, and the winter dust storms, or *harmattan*, challenge a pilot's stamina in flying Bible translators and nationals across the vast Liberian forests. Rugged dirt and grass airstrips add to the strain. But Ev and Carol have both adjusted during their two terms in Liberia.

The electrical outages often come without notice and last up to twelve hours. Carol will simply flex. She has kept a three-gallon container filled with ice water and will start cooking up food (to prevent spoilage) if the refrigerator loses power. Janel, Ben, and Steve have learned to accept Mom's almost-cool powdered milk at breakfast when the power fails. But sometimes they lose a loaf of bread to mold when it stays out of the refrigerator overnight. During their second term, the Smiths wired the house for twelve-volt battery power to drive the fans when the air conditioning shuts off. They recharge the batteries when the electricity returns.

Ev generally handles the heat well, though afternoon flights are difficult. "When I fly back in the afternoon, its 90 degrees outside and the sun is coming through the cockpit and it's hotter yet. It's bumpy and difficult to see where you're going because of dust. But that is part of the job."

Ev loves his job and has been at it—flying across sub-Saharan Liberia—for almost ten years. Prior to that he served JAARS in the Philippines for four years. Only recently has he returned to the United States on a home assignment as the Smiths seek medical treatment for their youngest son, Steve, who has suffered several Partial Complex Seizures. As Steve gets proper supervision and new medication, Evan is serving his fourth missionary term at JAARS headquarters in Waxhaw, North Carolina, where he is coordinator for recurrent training and instructs new JAARS pilots.

Ev hopes to return to Liberia once his son stabilizes and his older children are in college. Even an intermittent civil war in Liberia will not keep him away, for this is God's calling, and a vital work remains. Otherwise, he never would have gone to Liberia.

"If it wasn't for the impact of Bible translation and literacy, you'd be hard-pressed to find me over there flying. Sure, I'd go over there if the price was right—$60,000 a year, housing, paying for my children's education, and a trip home every year. But you couldn't pay me to do [this ministry]. I do it for the kingdom of God."

Ev arrived in Monrovia in 1980 at the request of officials at The Institute for Liberian Languages (TILL), an agency of Lutheran Bible Translators. TILL asked Wycliffe Bible Translators to run their aviation program after their own pilot had an accident. Jungle Aviation and Radio Service, Wycliffe's flying division, quickly responded. Wycliffe had stayed out of Liberia to respect the Lutheran Bible Translator's presence and avoid duplicated efforts. "But Wycliffe is on record as saying, 'We'll help anybody in any way we can,'" Ev notes.

As a result, pilots Ev and Roger Heiniger, along with two other JAARS pilots, a maintenance specialist, and their wives, are the only Wycliffe missionaries in Liberia. They serve most missionaries from their Monrovia base: Lutheran, Baptist, Methodist, and those from such mission groups as SIM International and New Tribes Mission.

For three and one-half years Ev was the sole pilot, averaging 540 hours each year, or forty-five flight hours a month. In medical emergencies, he airlifted missionaries and nationals alike, brought foodstuffs, and ferried

missionaries from remote villages to TILL for translation work.

The farthest missionaries he flew, Jim and Laura
Laesch, lived 360 miles from TILL in the village of Gee-
ken. The JAARS's Helio Courier shuttled them to Monrovia in one hour and forty-five minutes. It would have taken
eighteen hours to drive the winding road. They stay in the
villages several months translating the local language before returning to TILL to process their materials.

Dale and Alvina Federwitz, another translation team,
had no roads during their first nine years in a Bellah village. The Federwitzes have served Lutheran Bible Translators for twenty years, translating the Scriptures for the
Mandingo and Bellah groups. Finally, one year before
they finished translating the Bellah New Testament, a logging company cut the first dirt road into their village. They
can now drive 215 miles to TILL, but it requires eight
hours over bumpy dirt roads. "A straight line from their
village to TILL is only one hundred miles," Ev says. But
there are no straight lines. Rivers meander across the region and the Bellah Forest also prevents a clear path. Vehi-
cles average less than 30 MPH on the road. The Helio
Courier cuts their travel time by seven hours and "saves
lots of wear and tear on the missionaries," Ev says.

From December through early April, the *harmattan*—
dust storms caused by swirling winds—sweep across much
of Central Africa. Flying becomes tricky for Ev at that time.
Visibility can drop to zero in seconds. One dry season, Ev
flew nine consecutive weeks with one mile visibility. "That
is flyable, but it takes a lot of concentration" he says. "As
soon as it drops below one mile, we stop flying."

One year a severe *harmattan* forced Alvina Federwitz
and her children to walk instead of fly out of the village.
Dale had been at TILL meetings when he learned that one

of his children was sick. But the thick brown haze cut visibility to three hundred feet in the village, and none of the pilots could fly Dale to his family. After two days of walking, Alvina and the children met Dale, who was waiting on a logging road with a car. The Federwitzes would agree from personal experience: a plane makes a difference.

The JAARS pilots take special precautions during *harmattan* season. They clean the air filter after every flight, and the plane receives a thorough cleaning—from propeller to rudder—once a week. The blasted sand grains dust the plane lightly, leaving it coated with an African-style talcum powder. "You run your hand down the leading edge of the wing," Ev says, "and the dust will pile up."

---

*In Liberia, JAARS pilots cut
a missionary's schedule and fatigue in half.*

However, pilots find the heavy summer thunderstorms harder to handle. In four days during the 1988 summer, twenty-four inches of rain decended, Ev recalls. Roads washed out. Lakes appeared overnight, covering sections of road. Though water drained well from some dirt roads, car tires gouged ruts and mashed the mud, while trucks became mired and blocked traffic. Those roads, though not washed away, were impassable.

When the rains ceased, only planes could be counted on to get through. During September and October, everyone from missionaries to merchants besieged Ev and Roger Heiniger with requests for flights. The two Helio Couriers provided sure, quick travel that entire summer, when 240 inches of rain pummeled the Liberian coastal area in just four months.

In Liberia, JAARS pilots cut a missionary's schedule and fatigue in half. In trips to TILL and the shipping of food supplies, Lutheran missionaries Larry and Mae Johnson saved a lot of time—years, in fact. Larry once told Ev, "You saved me five years in preparing the Kisi New Testament."

"It wasn't that the translator wasn't a hard worker," Ev explains. "It's just all the twists and turns and potholes in those roads. In America if you want to travel 400 miles, you get in your car and, even at 50 MPH, you drive only eight hours. You drive a nice paved road, you're probably not fatigued—and you've had 7-Elevens all along the way where you can stop.

"Some people wonder whether driving in Liberia is such a big deal. In Africa, a twelve-hour drive is a big deal!" Ev exclaims. "It beats you to death. I've driven the roads, and the whole next day I'm tired, just from bouncing up and down. The airplane makes a difference."

In the mid-eighties, only 160 miles of roads were paved. The rest of Liberia's roads were dirt, often winding, routes with occasional ruts that assured a jostling ride. More paved roads appeared by 1990, but the recent civil war means that "the paved sections are probably deteriorating at a great rate," Ev says.

Ev stays above all those worrisome roads with his faithful Helio Courier, TILLY II. TILLY is a single-engine, high-wing airplane ideal for short takeoffs and landings (STOL). The plane's wings have leading-edge slats that make STOL flight easy. Like a commercial 727 jetliner, jutting slats during takeoff and landing allow the Helio Courier to attain a higher "angle of attack." The airplane lifts off more sharply from a shorter runway and lands in a shorter distance than most single-engine planes. Many Liberian airstrips are only one thousand feet long. A Cessna 185 or 206 can land on such strips, "but the safety margin is just not there," Ev says. "For the Helio, that's no problem at all."[1]

In all Liberia, only two airstrips are paved, both in Monrovia: the international airport and the city airport where the TILL planes are based. The rest are dirt or grass. "They go uphill, downhill—around the hills," Ev quips. A few have inclines of 10 percent, though most strips either start level, rising at the end, or are on a gradual incline. The Helio Courier's STOL capabilities ease tensions during takeoffs and landings.

TILLY II has other safety features pilots appreciate. "It is designed for passengers to survive a crash," Ev explains. The pilot and passengers are encased in a cabin he calls "a survivable container." Made of steel tubing, the cockpit can survive much stress. In addition to the energy-absorbing steel tubing, the plane will not stall in flight. The wings of most Cessna aircraft will cease flying in a stall condition, and the nose will pitch down. In contrast, the Helio Courier has a stabilator that limits the pitch to nineteen degrees. "The safety factor is greater. . . . If it's loaded properly, this plane will not cease to fly, and you have full control," Ev says. The plane will remain airborne at a mere thirty-five knots.

As a missionary pilot, Ev rarely does direct evangelism, but his ministry makes spiritual salvation possible. He assists the translators who will bring God's Word—and the message of salvation—to a new tribal group. "That is our ministry. When I save Larry and Mae Johnson five years on the translation, I minister to the people. In getting the Bellah New Testament to 80,000 Bellah people, I may not have helped directly with translation. But I helped the Federwitzes get it done much earlier than would have been possible otherwise."

His ministry extends to sustaining physical life. Ev remembers nine consecutive medical evacuations over several months where each person died. "That was discouraging," he admits. More often, however, medical emergencies have positive, even touching endings. He remembers Darrell Finley, a missionary who suspected he was suffering from malaria. After four days Finley felt so weak he asked a friend to help him drive to Monrovia, eighteen hours away. But various problems stymied their departure. "That was the Lord's hand!" declares Ev's wife, Carol.

Ev responded to their summons for a plane and delivered Finley to the Monrovia hospital in less than two hours. The resident surgeon quickly diagnosed Finley with having blood poisoning and began immediate treatment. The doctor told Ev two days later, "One more hour, and I would not have been able to save him."

Civil war. Those two words
cloud all of JAARS ministry in Liberia.

Carol dispels the idea that she and Ev are missionaries because they are good people. "Some think we must be superhuman or at least extra-spiritual . . . or maybe just good people. The truth is we are here simply because there is a job to do and God has directed us, at this time, to serve him here," she wrote supporters while in Liberia.[2] "We remain thoroughly convinced that *through the Scriptures*, answers can be found for *all* of life's questions. 'Why did God give us life? How can we handle sin?' And herein is the explanation of God's love shown for us through Jesus Christ— He being the *only* path to a life united with God."

In March 1987, Ev carried a special cargo to the Kisi tribal people: the book of Matthew, a pre-primer, and a storybook. The following year the entire Kisi New Testament was completed and ready for the printers. It will be a valuable tool to bring spiritual salvation to the Kisi, a west Africa people with their own local government and many businesspeople. The Kisi economy blends commerce with agriculture. The Kisi grow rice and rarely face drought or food shortages in this semi-developed culture. Yet they have no running water and minimal electricity.

When Matthew was delivered, about seven hundred villagers could read it, Evan estimates. The primer and storybook will lead thousands more villagers to literacy. Several thousand Kisi live in the area, and more than one million live throughout Liberia and into Sierra Leone and French New Guinea. (Four dialects are spoken.)

Ev recalls that cargo load with excitement. "That's where it's at for us. We're in the business of Bible translation and literacy. I wouldn't be over there working otherwise. Someone may say, 'Well, you didn't have anything to do with that New Testament or those primers.' But remember the missionary [Larry Johnson] who told me he completed the New Testament five years sooner because the airplane was available. That means five years' worth of more people will have the Scriptures. I don't know how many Kisi people die in five years. But if they lose 20,000 people, that's 20,000 more who now have a chance to hear the gospel. That's why I do it."

That good news is tempered by two words that have dominated Liberia in the early 1990s: civil war. Those two words cloud all of JAARS ministry in Liberia. Translators and pilots had anticipated that the Kisi New Testament would be printed within six months, but the war has delayed its delivery. And the primers are not used much when the people are thinking of survival.

"Before the civil war the Kisi literacy program was going well in several villages," Ev reports. "The civil war has brought that to a halt. It is a shame." Famine, an alien word to most of Liberia, now appears in parts of the country.

The civil war has disrupted much evangelical work. Smith and other missionaries were stunned when the rebels invaded the ELWA mission compound owned by SIM. The army destroyed one-third of the compound, wrecking the printing press, transmitters, and radio studios. They spared the hospital and the pharmacy, but toppled about 20 percent of the houses, Ev estimates. SIM missionaries have since returned to run the hospital.

"The civil war has just about devastated the country," Ev says. Fighting has shattered the infrastructure, and Ev believes it will require five years before all electricity returns. Monrovia water mains have hundreds of breaks. If officials opened the water to the whole city, they would lose 60 percent of the flow through those ruptures, according to Ev.

The interim government has been challenged by the chief rebel leader, Charles Taylor, who in 1991 controlled half the population and 90 percent of the land.[3] "He has the whole country tied up, and . . . he keeps the people from coming from the interior. They're sick and malnourished."

Pilots can fly only into Monrovia now; anywhere else in Liberia they would be simply dodging and weaving through a combat zone. Evan returned briefly to Monrovia from JAARS's U.S. headquarters in 1991 to survey the scene and help other JAARS pilots there. He was told of ten- and twelve-year-old boys carrying automatic weapons, shooting randomly. "There isn't a power line in Monrovia that doesn't have a hole in it," he says. "At one time probably more than a half million shell casings lay between our hangar and the main airport terminal. There were so many you slipped on them."

Though he now serves at JAARS's home office, Ev has returned to Liberia as needed for several six-week visits.

When his son Steve recovers and their three children are settled, Carol and he will return.

"We'd go back quickly. The civil war has tripled the amount of things that need to be done. There was enough to do in literacy and translation before the war. The civil war has brought inflation. The farmers have been unable to plant crops for two years. There is little food except what the UN provided. Many are sick, and there's malnutrition. There is also much hate because of all the atrocities."

Evan Smith's goal is like every missionary pilot's: to bring the gospel to the remote parts of the earth.

Ev expects that road bandits will roam the roads even after the war ends, and children with guns may remain a problem. With road travel unsafe, missionaries, church leaders, and villagers will need the JAARS airservice even more.

"The only thing that will settle this situation permanently will be for all Liberians to get hold of the Word of God in their own language," Ev concludes. "They have had English for two hundred years, with missionaries preaching to them. They still don't understand it. Get the gospel in their own language, and they will have the vision and can understand and make a decision.

"The goal is obtainable. God's Word in everybody's language is obtainable; 100 percent evangelization of a language group may not be. That makes this work really exciting."

Evangelization. Evan Smith's goal is like every missionary pilot's: to bring the gospel to the remote parts of the earth. For five decades, Christian pilots have continued to do that. They are part of a heritage that includes pioneers such as Nate Saint and Betty Greene. How this vision took wing is an exciting story, and we will see it unfold in the chapters to follow.

Notes

1. The JAARS fleet includes several Cessna airplanes. The Cessna is equal to the Helio Courier in airworthiness and effectiveness, a JAARS spokesperson emphasized. On a very short runway (five hundred to twelve hundred feet) the Helio Courier has a greater safety margin, but the Cessna also has STOL capabilities and handles airstrips as short as twelve hundred feet with little difficulty. The chief advantages of the Cessna are that it holds more cargo and travels faster than the Helio Courier. Both types of aircraft are respected and well used in missionary aviation.
2. JAARS newsletter from Evan and Carol Smith, June 1987.
3. Telephone interview with Evan Smith, May 2, 1991.

6

A Vision Takes Wing

The former Army Air Corps crew chief lowered a canvas bucket over the side of his plane and slowly let out the long line. As the plane gently circled in the Ecuadorian sky, the spiraling line moved in a smaller and smaller arc. As the arc flattened, Nate Saint lowered the plane, and eventually the bucket reached the end of an invisible inverted cone and hung motionless in a straight line. The pilot eased his small cargo gently to the ground.

Now the awaiting missionary could easily remove the goods while the pilot, unable to land in the small space, circled safely above. Saint used this system to deliver wire for communication, convey medicine and other supplies, and lower gifts to an otherwise unapproachable tribe of Indians. The bucket drop was only one of several innovations Nate Saint brought to a fledgling Christian ministry—missionary aviation.

An earlier invention has since saved the lives of many pilots and missionaries. Saint had heard about a plane crash caused by a failure in the fuel system. Though the Gospel Missionary Union pilot and a passenger survived, Saint did not want the scene to repeat itself. So he designed an alternate fuel system: improvising with his wife's cooking oil tins and a copper tube with a valve he could open from the side, Saint released spare fuel from the tins down a strut to the engine. Nate's invention was a boon to jungle flying and earned the young pilot a U.S. patent after the Civil Aeronautics Administration approved his invention.[1]

Nate Saint was one of the earliest pilots for Mission Aviation Fellowship, and certainly its most creative. In six months he rebuilt the mission's first and only plane after it crashed in Mexico, even though he found the wing tips stuck in a bushel basket and had no hangar to store tools or protect himself during the long days in the tropical sun.[2] Nate also developed a parachute device to drop large quantities of canned goods. But his greatest contribution to missionary aviation came on a desolate sand bar on the Curaray River in Ecuador, where his bucket drops had prepared the way for the visit of five missionaries, including Saint, on January 2, 1956.

For three months Nate had lowered gifts in his flying bucket to the Auca Indians, a savage tribe no one had seen but that air reconnaissance showed to be there. His first gift was a small aluminum kettle containing twenty brightly colored buttons. He attached colorful ribbon streamers to fifteen of the buttons. Nate explained in his diary that the buttons were "obviously not for their clothes since they didn't wear any, but they do make good ornaments."[3] Nate made twelve more drops, one each week, leaving machetes, kettles, shirts, trousers, and more trinkets.

After the first drop of ribbon-festooned buttons, Nate concluded his diary entry for the day: "At present we feel unanimously that God is in it. May the praise be His and may it be that some Auca, clothed in the righteousness of Jesus Christ, will be with us as we lift our voice in praise before His throne. Amen."[4]

Finally Nate and missionary Ed McCully dropped photos of themselves and three other missionaries to prepare the Aucas for the arrival of the first white men to tell about a God who loved them. To help identify themselves as the source of the airborne gifts, each missionary held gifts, and two of the photos also featured drawings of planes.

McCully landed on January 2, and in the next three days, Saint flew missionaries Jim Elliot, Roger Youderian, and Peter Fleming to the sand-bar beach. One day later three Auca, an older woman, a teen-age girl, and a man about twenty, came to the riverbank. An elated Elliot led the three to the sand bar and his missionary friends, and the three Indians stayed all afternoon. They were animated, and when the young warrior showed interest in the Piper plane, Nate decided to take him up. Afterward the excited Auca asked for a second ride. At twilight the three quietly slipped into the jungle.[5]

The missionaries were jubilant about their first meeting with the Auca and broadcast their success back to the mission base camp. Two days later, on Sunday, the five men were singing hymns when they saw about ten Indians headed for the beach. The missionaries radioed the news back to their station and said they would call back as soon as they had something to report. That was their final transmission.[6]

Within one day, radio station HCJB was beaming an international report about the five martyrs. The station reported that a helicopter rescue team had spotted four bodies. When the ground party arrived, they found that the four men, including Nate Saint, had been speared. Ed McCully lay nearby, dead from machete wounds. Draped over the shaft of one spear were the pierced pages of a Bible.[7] Three weeks later *Life* magazine printed a complete story. In its lead article, the weekly magazine recounted the final days of the five missionaries, displayed the five photos of the men holding their gifts, pictures of two of the slain men, the widows and their children, and excerpts from Nate's diary.

The American people's response was heartfelt. Most regarded them as genuine martyrs and felt sadness for the wives and children left fatherless. Hundreds of young men and women dedicated themselves to missions, and Nate's example made people aware of the dedication of missionary pilots, inspiring dozens to train to be missionary fliers.

Some, however, questioned the missionaries' judgment in contacting the Auca. Recently Nate's older sister Rachel recalled the event: "The men had taken a calculated risk and lost—or so it seemed. But had they? Their objective was to open the door for the gospel to those who had never heard of a God of love who sent His Son to save them. What they hoped to accomplish with their lives, in God's economy they accomplished in their deaths."[8]

She was right. Their zeal kindled a passion for missions among many young people and brought to the Auca life everlasting. Rachel, herself a missionary studying the Auca language, reached the village two years later, along with Jim Elliot's widow, Elizabeth. Two Auca girls had come to the station and invited the women back. They explained that the Auca tribesmen had killed the five, fearing the white men were cannibals; but the warriors would not kill women. So the two women came, and several months later the leader of the brutal attack, Gikita, became a Christian when he realized the five men came in love. "They loved God and they loved you, and said they would die first," Rachel told Gikita. He was among the first believers in a village that now is largely Christian.[9]

Nate's wish that "some Auca, clothed in the righteousness of Jesus Christ, will be with us . . ." had been answered. Meanwhile, his courage in a hostile jungle helped missionary aviation take off. A vision took wing, bringing new pilots, prayer support, and financial assistance to a relatively new enterprise.

The first aviation ministry
to serve missionaries in several countries
began as World War II ended.

Since then, the missionary pilot has lifted the missionary enterprise and its goal—evangelizing the world for Jesus Christ—to new heights. As missions expert Ruth Tucker declares in her classic textbook *From Jerusalem to Irian Jaya*, "Missionary aviation has revolutionized Christian missions in the past several decades. The weeks and months of arduous travel have become a phenomenon of the past, and no longer do isolated missionaries in remote villages endure for months at a time without needed health services, fresh food, and mail deliveries. Today a single MAF pilot covers as much territory in six weeks as David Livingstone covered in a lifetime of African exploration, and with much less strain on his health and family relationships."[10]

The first aviation ministry to serve missionaries in several countries began as World War II ended. In 1945 Christian Airmen's Missionary Fellowship (CAMF) began when three Navy fliers realized that the time and energy saving device that the military used in moving troops and supplies to the war front—the airplane—could aid missionary soldiers in another quest—the battle for men's spiritual lives.

CAMF, soon to become Mission Aviation Fellowship, took off after several earlier solo missionary efforts flew with mixed success. The U.S. Marine Corps was indirectly involved in the first known flight of a missionary in 1924. A Marine officer flew Harry Carson, an Episcopal missionary in Haiti, across the country for pastoral ministry. Another one-time flight in Alaska three years later involved a second Episcopal missionary, Peter Rowe. Both trips were briefly planned, one-time events.[11]

The same year as Rowe's flight, a Presbyterian missionary of the Australian Inland Mission had a pilot fly a doctor into the Australian Outback to treat a miner with a broken pelvis and then shuttle the patient to a hospital. The missionary, John Flynn, had pilots help him bring in medical aid on a regular basis in 1933, when the program was named the Australian Aerial Medical Service (AAMS). This regular program of medical flights represents the first missions aviation program,[12] though it was limited to one country. AAMS transported doctors to patients, who gave medical aid as Flynn gave spiritual comfort.

AAMS grew, helped when a young engineer developed a new radio receiver to let patients notify the doctor during emergencies. Renamed the Flying Doctors Service in 1942, the organization was praised by Queen Elizabeth in 1955, who granted the prefix "Royal" to the agency. An obelisk to Flynn includes the words "He brought to the lonely places a spiritual ministry, and spread a mantle of safety over them by medicine, aviation and radio." The Royal Flying Doctors Service continues today, though the spiritual ministry has been forsaken as government sponsorship has increased.[13]

Two evangelical missionaries were pioneering pilots. Paul B. F. Carlson of the Evangelical Mission Covenant Church began air service in western Alaska in 1939. Financial gifts from the Covenant Church, and especially its young people, paid for a Fairchild 24 plane. On his first trip Carlson flew along the Yukon Delta to White Horse, skirting Alaska's western coast. The trip of more than six hundred miles took five and one-half hours and cost only $55, about one-seventh the bill of dog-sled travel and requiring about one week less time than the dog sled.[14] Later he flew a Piper Cruiser between congregations in Alaska. Raould Amundsen, another Covenant pilot, shared flight duties and later started the Missionary Aircraft Repair Center, still active in Alaska.[15]

CAMF organized to provide pilots for many existing missions and sent its first plane to Wycliffe Bible Translators. Its first pilot was Betty Greene.

An American in the South Pacific would finally prod mission aviation beyond a haphazard, mission-pilot-here, mission-pilot-there routine. Rev. George Fisk concluded that a plane was essential to reach efficiently his "wild men of Borneo."[16] However, his mission, the Christian and Missionary Alliance (CMA), rejected his proposal the first time. The CMA finally agreed in 1939 to provide a plane, and Fisk began flights that year. He developed the aviation program for the CMA and then passed the plane on to Fred Jackson. Unfortunately, Japanese soldiers in Borneo killed Jackson and destroyed the plane during World War II.

Fisk no longer had a plane, but he had a vision. He returned from Borneo and told U.S. churches about his experiences, and from pulpits and aviation magazine stories he called for pilots to become the ally of the missionary.[17] It was natural and necessary for missionaries to soar on wings in ministry for God's kingdom.

Lt. James Lomheim, a Navy pilot, heard Fisk's pleas to help the CMA restore its flight operation, and he discussed with other Christian military veterans the need for pilots to help in the missionary enterprise. One of the servicemen, Navy pilot Jim Truxton, had read an article in *His* magazine by Women's Airforce Service Pilot (WASP) Elizabeth Greene describing the need to fly airplanes for missions and her plans to help. Truxton agreed with Lomheim and others,[18] and in May 1945 they formed the Christian Airmen's Missionary Fellowship (CAMF).

CAMF organized to provide pilots for many existing missions and sent its first plane to Wycliffe Bible Translators. Its first pilot was Betty Greene, the WASP flier whose magazine article inspired Truxton to pursue mission aviation. Within a year Truxton and others renamed CAMF the Missionary Aviation Fellowship, as they began to seek pilots outside the military. By 1971 MAF would be called simply Mission Aviation Fellowship, reflecting its ministry to national churches as well.

As MAF's first pilot, Betty brought aboard impeccable credentials. Like the founders, she was a flying veteran of World War II. She had flown radar missions and later helped in developmental projects, flying a B-17 bomber at 35,000 feet. She helped test flying suits and oxygen masks in the open fuselage. Her magazine article calling for pilots to join in aiding missionaries had prompted Truxton to send her a letter. "Some of us men in the military are forming such an organization," he wrote. "Will you help us?"[19]

Betty quickly came to MAF's California headquarters and after a year flew a Waco biplane into Tuxtla, Mexico, site of Wycliffe Bible Translators' jungle camp program. Here Wycliffe prepared missionaries for jungle living, and here Wycliffe founder Cameron Townsend soon asked Betty to help the mission in Peru. Almost thirty years of active service followed as the MAF pilot helped various mission agencies in South America, Africa, and Indonesia.

With a large war-surplus Grumman Duck, an amphibian plane with a 1,000-horsepower engine, Betty soared above 18,000 feet while clearing the Peruvian Andes Mountains. Also in Peru, she had her first engine failure. With a military officer aboard, she pointed the craft to the nearby Napo River after the engine quit. "I maneuvered the amphibian plane over the river in hopes of landing on the water," Betty recalls. "The plane was dropping very rapidly. Up ahead, just about where we wanted to land, was a sharp curve in the river. We needed to clear the curve in order to land safely, but we didn't seem to have momentum to get past it. Suddenly, the engine caught on just long enough for us to clear the curve and then it quit again.

"I was able to land the Grumman on the river without any difficulty at all. While I was still in my cockpit, the officer in the cockpit behind me jumped out and stood on the wing beside me. He yelled (in Spanish), 'What's the matter with you, senorita? Why are you so calm?'

"But I thought it was marvelous. We were safe! I knew that the Lord had intervened to protect us."[20]

Betty retained that assurance throughout her thirty years of flying with MAF, helping various mission groups to share the gospel and bring spiritual and physical aid. During her final overseas assignment in Irian Jaya, she discovered personally the difference planes were making in a missionary's ministry and well-being. Before flying to one outpost, she had to complete a long, rough jungle trek to inspect a new airstrip. The strip had been built specifically for the MAF plane; now Betty had to determine if it was safe for an actual takeoff and landing. She could not risk the craft, so the only way in was a thirty-mile walk.

She joined another female missionary and eight Moni tribesmen who acted as carriers for the overland trip. Betty's hearty missionary friend, Leona St. John, hiked across the frayed vine bridges and the slippery mud embankments with slight effort, and the eight carriers were used to the daily tropical rainstorms. But Betty struggled.

"I didn't know how hard it would be," she recalls. "I suppose the carriers were perfectly aware of the trail, but for most of the way I didn't even think there was one. The place we were going was supposed to be thirty walking miles away, but I think the map meant horizontal miles, and most of ours were straight up and straight down."[21]

Betty soon understood how her plane could save the missionary time, energy, and safety. Those lessons of lives saved and missionary ministries prolonged typify mission aviation's history. In fact, only a few years before Betty arrived, two tragic incidents had forced missions agencies to see the need for planes to help their missionaries.

In 1939 Walter Herron left the Bolivian Indian Mission a widower after his wife of one year died in childbirth. Herron needed five days to transport his wife, Violet, to the hospital via ox cart and boat, and his wife never recovered from complications. As the despondent missionary left Bolivia, pushing his newborn son in an ox cart, he heard a plane overhead and said aloud to a friend, "That's what I need! If I only had had a plane like that, Violet would probably be with us today. It would have been no problem at all to have taken her to Trinidad [in Bolivia]."[22]

Herron tried to develop an aviation service for Bolivian missionaries while back in Australia, his native country, but was unsuccessful. So he decided to leave his infant son in New Zealand with his wife's parents and travel to the United States to speak at American churches to raise funds for a plane. Within one year he had his pilot's license and

Nate Saint holds an early version of his bucket-drop system, later used to drop gifts to Auca tribesmen in Ecuador and gain entry for missionaries.

MAF's Betty Greene poses in front of the massive Grumman Duck that she flew into Peru to help Wycliffe Bible Translators.

Years later, the versatile Greene repairs another airplane while serving in the Sudan.

MAF Pilot Josue Balderas celebrates the acquisition of a Cessna 206 aircraft as MAF president Max Meyers listens.

Josue has served in Oaxaca, Mexico, two terms with his wife, Lynn, and their two children.

Meanwhile, John and Cora Lou Miller have been MAF missionaries in Irian Jaya for almost twenty years.

Karen and Dave Neinhuis and their sons take a vacation break as Dave continues his strong recovery.

JAARS pilot Evan Smith flies his Helio Courier across Liberia, Africa.

Several Piper airplanes line up on the grass airfield at Wood Dale Airport, part of Moody Bible Institute's missionary aviation training program in the 1950s.

Paul Robinson (front seat) and Paul Wertheimer, director of flight training, prepare to demonstrate Nate Saint's bucket-drop technique.

Four seniors move to their planes for afternoon training flights.

With Moody Aviation director Paul Robinson in the cockpit, students push a ski-equipped aircraft into place for takeoff on the snow-covered airfield.

On a warmer spring day, Robinson diagrams a flight path as students plan their annual cross-country flight.

Unable to become a missionary pilot himself, Paul Robinson started Moody Aviation and sent many in his place, including these eleven MAF pilots in Brazil, whom he calls "my boys."

Bob Rich, director of maintenance training, explains technique as students practice welding procedures.

Flight instructor Ed Robinson continues his father's love of missionary flying, teaching student pilots at Moody Aviation.

Today, students such as Bryan Lorch and John Mosby perform 100-hour service inspections on aircraft engines as part of their training.

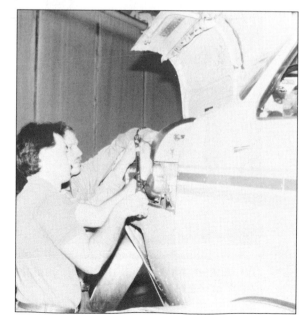

Moody flight instructor Ron Royce verifies the fuel dipstick level as part of preflight inspection before Dan Morgan begins his maiden flight in a Cessna 185.

Clif Jensen, ABWE pilot in Brazil, completes a preflight check in the predawn hour.

left on a ship for Bolivia with a Piper J-5 Cub aboard, thanks to gifts from American Christians.

Herron's story of his wife's suffering during five long days of travel by cart and boat moved one pastor so deeply that he determined he would become a pilot and go to the mission field to prevent more deaths. Paul Robinson, a Baptist pastor in western New York, took lessons and so-loed in early December 1941, intent on being a missionary pilot. But four days later the United States entered World War II, and Robinson joined the Civil Air Patrol. Mission service would have to await war's end. However, the war continued almost four years, and Robinson, now thirty-five, was deemed too old to serve.

Paul Robinson launched the first
specific missionary aviation course
at Moody Bible Institute in Chicago.

Though deeply disappointed, Robinson was still convinced that God wanted him involved in missionary aviation and that the airplane would be a significant tool in the worldwide spread of the gospel. Eventually he decided that if he could not go himself he would train other Christian pilots to take his place. He knew about the newly organized Christian Airmen's Missionary Fellowship, asked about their needs, and began to consider the needs of other missions agencies. Within a year, Paul Robinson launched the first specific missionary aviation course at Moody Bible Institute in Chicago. The missionary technical course today is known as Moody Aviation, the longest active missionary flight school in the country.[23]

Meanwhile, Herron returned to Bolivia under tough conditions. Though the Piper J-5 had been test flown, it was hardly broken in. The recommended ceiling for a Piper with a new engine was only 12,600 feet, and some of his flights required climbing above 12,000-foot mountains. Herron lessened his risk by departing on his "high mountain days" at 4:00 A.M., when the smoother, cooler air would least burden the plane. He would leave his airport at 9,000 feet, and sometimes he would circle at the ceiling level to burn off fuel and lighten the plane before his final climb over the Andes.

His adventures were all successful, and he did not have a single accident in twenty-two years of flying on evangelistic trips and bringing other missionaries supplies, mail, and medical aid. The Piper would be the first plane in an aviation program that continues today as the Andes Evangelical Mission. Eventually the Bolivian government gave Herron its highest award—the Condor of the Andes.[24]

The second event forcing mission agencies to look to aviation for help involved Wycliffe founder Cameron Townsend. As early as 1929 he had contacted an Army Air Corp pilot and discussed the practicality of starting an aviation ministry to assist Wycliffe missionaries in South America. The pilot had flown in South America and offered sound advice, and a confident Townsend recommended WBT establish an aviation arm. However, the WBT board of directors turned him down due to the high costs.

Now in 1947, Cam, his wife, and their baby daughter boarded a small plane in a mission outpost for a flight to Mexico City. Shortly after takeoff their inexperienced Mexican pilot turned back over the jungle, unable to gain proper altitude. After barely missing some tall trees, the plane smashed into a ravine, shearing off a wing and landing on its side. Cam was able to free himself from the wreckage despite a broken leg; then he helped his wife and daughter escape. He surveyed the scene as he waited for his rescuers: though his daughter was unharmed, his wife had a severely lacerated left foot, and the pilot was badly injured. He decided that WBT must develop it own efficient aviation support agency with specially trained pilots who could assist his jungle-based translators.[25]

Most board members still resisted the idea and pointed to the growing contribution of MAF, which had helped them just a year earlier by sending Betty Greene to Peru. "Let MAF do it," several members were saying. Townsend knew MAF was aiding many missions by now and could not meet all WBT's needs. He concluded that Wycliffe *had* to have missionary pilots because of the hazards of jungle ministry. Later, two male translators were almost drowned in river rapids, and WBT translators craved air service to receive prompt delivery of medicines and other supplies. "We are in aviation (by being in the jungle) whether we like it or not," he told the board. He decided to organize a mission aviation branch despite the board's reservations.[26]

Jungle Aviation and Radio Service (JAARS) began with one plane to serve WBT, and like Mission Aviation Fellowship, JAARS brought its first pilot from the military. Forty years later it has thirty-two aircraft in eight countries. Only MAF, with eighty-seven aircraft, has more. The two agencies are among forty involved in mission aviation. Some of these organizations are aviation branches of large nondenominational agencies, others serve denominational mission agencies, and still others are specialized aviation agencies such as Mission Aviation and Repair Center, which helps Alaskan aviators, and Helimission, which operates a fleet of eight helicopters.

Together they have revolutionized Christian missions, according to Tucker. It is a welcome revolution. On the following pages you will meet some of the men and women who have been part of it.

Notes

1. Dale M. Brown, ed. *The Bush Pilots* (New York: Time-Life Books, 1983), pp. 137-38.
2. Russell T. Hitt, *Jungle Pilot: The Life and Witness of Nate Saint* (New York: Harper & Brothers, 1959), pp. 113, 117, 125. (The book was subsequently published by Zondervan in 1973.)
3. "'Go Ye and Preach the Gospel.' Five Do and Die," *Life*, January 30, 1956, p.12.
4. Ibid.
5. Brown, *The Bush Pilots*, p. 139.
6. Ibid., p. 140.
7. Ibid.
8. Rachel Saint, "Operation Auca: Thirty-five years Later," *The Gospel Message*, no. 2 (1991), p. 4.
9. Ibid.
10. Ruth Tucker, *From Jerusalem to Irian Jaya* (Grand Rapids: Zondervan, 1983), p. 395.
11. John David Kendrick, "Historical Survey of Christian Aviation Ministries," unpublished doctoral diss. (August 1, 1985), pp. 6-7.
12. John Wells and Glenn Arnold, "Winging the Word," *Christian Herald* (September 1981), p. 55.
13. Kendrick, "Historical Survey," pp. 9-11.
14. Ibid., p. 16.
15. John Wells, "Missionaries, Needs, and Aircraft," transcript from slide presentation, Archives of the Billy Graham Center, Wheaton College, Wheaton, Illinois.
16. Wells and Arnold, "Winging the Word," p. 55.
17. Ibid., pp. 55-56.
18. Jim Buyers and Clarence Soderberg joined Truxton in a meeting with evangelist Jack Wyrtzen in New York. That meeting led to the formation of CAMF.
19. Lee Roddy, *On Wings of Love* (Nashville: Thomas Nelson, 1981), pp. 15-16.
20. Betty Greene, "Pilot with a Mission," *Decision* (May 1991), p. 27.
21. Mary Wade, "On a Wing and a Prayer," *The Saturday Evening Post* (April 1980), p. 105.
22. Wells and Arnold, "Winging the Word," p. 56.

23. The program began in 1946 and continues to send 80 percent of its flight alumni into missions service. The Paul Robinson story begins in chapter 7.
24. Kendrick, "Historical Survey," pp. 23-24.
25. Tucker, *From Jerusalem*, pp. 401-2.
26. Ibid., p. 402.

7

Pastor, Pilot, and Pioneer

The evangelist wanted to introduce his family before he began his message. He invited them to the platform of the Baptist church and placed his little six-year-old, Paul, on the podium for everyone to see.

"Paul, do you love Jesus?" Dad asked.

Gazing out at 250 people from his podium perch, the six-year-old felt on the spot. So he just nodded his head up and down, saying nothing.

"The setting wasn't exactly to my choosing," Paul Robinson recalls. "I wasn't a public speaker at the time."

Almost thirty years later Paul still didn't feel the poised, gifted public speaker as he faced a much smaller but slightly more impressive group. He stood before the Board of Trustees at Moody Bible Institute (MBI) in Chicago, trying to sell them a vision. He wanted the school to help him inaugurate a program to train pilots to serve missionaries worldwide. It was a novel idea and would bring several questions from the interested yet cautious ten men seated before him.

Paul later told a reporter, "I was only a country preacher from the boonies in the presence of those great men of God."[1] But the men were "kind, gracious, and sympathetic," Paul adds, and he quickly felt he was at home among friends. They listened with increasing enthusiasm to a novel plan from a man with unusual vision.

His vision for mission aviation took off after he heard about the Bolivian missionary whose pregnant wife died unable to reach the hospital in time. "Wally Herron had tried desperately to get his pregnant wife to a hospital after complications. They took her by ox cart to the river bank, and for several days she sat in a dug-out canoe as they brought her to a hospital. This dear woman needed more than medicine. She needed transportation."

"We should wait no longer," Paul told his wife, Lillian. "I'm ready to go to the mission field, whether by land, sea, or air."

News of Herron's loss convinced Paul that he must become a missionary pilot. Years earlier a Baptist missionary on furlough from Brazil had told him about the need for air transportation. "It was obvious to me how a plane would help in Brazil's Amazon. Rubber hunters and missionaries both worked in these almost impenetrable jungles. The hunters were ruthless, the missionaries selfless. The latter needed help."

As a young New York pastor, Paul had caught a vision for international missions. Hearing the story of this missionary couple, he now felt he should combine his love of flying with missions. "For some time I had thought that a light airplane, now available at a reasonable cost, might overcome some of those jungle barriers."

He felt he had to act quickly. "We should wait no longer," Paul told his wife, Lillian. "I'm ready to go to the mission field, whether by land, sea, or air." Paul began to pray about finding a way and wondered where to enroll at a flight school and how he could pay for the costly lessons.

"God has means," says the pastor who would be pilot. A wealthy businessman who had purchased three Piper Cruisers, one for each of his children, heard about Paul's plans. He kept one based at nearby Perth Airport and offered free use. The Cruiser was an ideal plane for training, and Paul soon began his flying lessons with a Perth instructor. Weeks passed, and Paul was ready to solo. He performed well, pleasing his instructor, and imagined that his days in missions skies were not far off. He planned to help in Brazil, but his field would not be the valleys and villages alone. He would reach to the clouds where God's faithfulness extended (Psalm 36:5).

Four days after his solo flight, however, the Japanese bombed Pearl Harbor. The next day the United States entered World War II, and all civilian aviation was grounded. Mission fields closed as well, and Paul decided to join the Civil Air Patrol, a civilian group that used their airplanes to assist the war effort. He could continue his training, but what about Brazil? "The war came along and knocked that plan in the head," he says. "My plans, which I thought were God's plans, were dashed."

As the war continued, he took a new pastorate in Forestville, New York, accepting the delay and continuing his flying. The Robinsons found much comfort here, for Forestville Baptist Church, only forty miles from Buffalo, was the same Baptist church in which Paul's father preached as a traveling evangelist. Rev. Paul Robinson now stood *behind* the same podium that he once had stood *upon* as a six-year-old. Meanwhile, Lillian discovered that the parsonage was the same one her mother had lived in as a child. Lillian's grandpa had once been the pastor in the same parish that Lillian's husband now led.

Three years later they learned about a great need that would push them from this comfortable setting. As co-founder of the American Mission for Opening Closed Churches (AMOC), Paul heard about the Village Church, an abandoned church in Mount Morris, not far from Forestville. The church had stood empty for twenty years but was in good repair, including its fine pipe organ. As the Robinsons toured the small town of 12,000, they learned that the community was largely Catholic and that the three Protestant churches were weak. Each lacked a full-time minister. The mission found no pastor ready to answer the need. Would the Robinsons help?

"It would mean giving up my church, forgoing my salary, moving to Mount Morris, and trying to find suitable housing," Paul says. AMOC agreed to sponsor the project and purchase the property. And Paul agreed to open the church and spend one year in establishing a ministry. He raised financial and prayer support by visiting friends and missions-minded churches.

"I was amazed at the way the Lord met our needs. Even the house we rented was special. A plaque in the front read 'This was the house where Francis Bellamy, author of the pledge to the American flag, was born and lived.' I'm patriotic, and that was special."

They put notices in the local newspaper, and several families who wanted to be at a Bible teaching church decided to help in promotion. After twenty years with its doors closed, the Village Church opened on Sunday morning, June 10, 1945, with eighty-five people. Within a couple weeks they had their first converts. The Shurtleffs had attended another Protestant church many years without hearing the gospel. "The Holy Spirit had them ready," Paul says. "The first minute they heard the gospel, Christ touched their hearts."

The church had revived after being closed almost twenty years, and it echoed the revival Paul led at Louisiana State University during his student days. Although he attended Baptist Student Union (BSU) activities and a local Baptist church with several BSU members, he rebelled when the BSU left a slip in his campus mailbox one Monday morning asking him to help in their evening program the next Sunday. He was a nominal Christian—and he knew it—and did not want to be exposed. He planned to go to the BSU office to decline the assignment after his class.

But during the class "I came under conviction. I forgot what the prof said that morning, but I heard the voice of the Lord. In several ways during that class hour, God said to me, 'Paul, you are at the crossroads. If you refuse to go down there Sunday night, you've had it.' Finally I said, 'All right, I surrender.'"

He returned to his room, began reading his Bible, and "spent the entire morning talking to the Lord. I was well versed in Scripture but not surrendered to the Lord. I got down on my knees, confessed my sin, and had it out with the Lord. By the end of that day I was ready for Sunday night."

That Sunday night he stood up when his turn came to read the Scripture. "I'm not going to read this, but I have something to say." He told of his rebellion and his return to God. "The result was electrifying," Paul says. "Several other students took a stand. They confessed their sins and said they were worldly Christians. Many things got straightened out right there. Revival spread to the campus," Robinson says, as BSU members invited an evangelist to preach one week. He spoke at a local auditorium five nights, and each night Robinson gave his testimony. Many college students came to Christ. Afterward, the BSU organized Bible studies, classes, and gospel teams. Paul played his trumpet as a member of one team.

As CAMF continued to organize,
soon to become
Mission Aviation Fellowship,
Robinson recognized the need
for training missionaries.

Now he was pastor of the revived Village Church. Though Paul was excited, he agreed to stay only one year; the war was winding down, and he thought countries might soon swing open their doors again to missionaries. During the year he sought to prepare the congregation for its next pastor. "Paul has good vision," Lillian explains "He would start a work but he always would look for someone to follow him and take over the work."

Paul was ready to start a new work. But he could no longer be a missionary. The four years of war left him too old in the eyes of mission agencies. Though he looked once more to Brazil, numerous mission boards refused to approve him for service. "Robinson turned to the next best option. He would teach potential missionaries to fly."[2]

He now had his private and commercial licenses and was qualified as a flight instructor. He heard about a fledgling organization, Christian Airmen's Missionary Fellowship, that wanted to use their skills to fly missionaries in remote areas. He contacted the leaders and became a charter member—in fact, number twelve on the membership list—joining others in praying for and promoting mission aviation. As CAMF continued to organize, soon to become Mission Aviation Fellowship, Robinson recognized the need for training missionaries. He had recently visited with Henry C. Crowell, MBI executive vice president, to tell him about his desire to start a program. They had had conversations ten years earlier, as Paul completed the Pastor's Course at the school. Then they had talked about their mutual interests in aviation. Now Crowell listened with interest to Robinson's commitment to mission aviation and prompted him to "keep at it."

Paul did keep at it, and that fall an idea took root and began to germinate. "I was helping Lillian dry dishes one evening when the whole panorama of an aviation training program unfolded in my mind. I dropped the towel, went to the desk, and began to write. I wrote most of the night and all the next day, until I thought I had it.

"I was now ready to offer my prospectus to a good school. I decided to start at the top. And I never got off the top. Moody Bible Institute was my first choice." He submitted his proposal to MBI in February 1946, during the school's annual Founder's Week Bible conference. Crowell had been the key man in developing Moody radio broadcasting and the Moody Institute of Science, two pioneering evangelistic programs, and he listened intently. The MBI officials seemed pleased during their initial interviews but needed more time to evaluate the proposal.

Though excited about a possible training program, Paul now had a complicated decision. David Weyerhauser, part of the Weyerhauser lumber company in Tacoma, Washington, knew about Paul's missionary zeal and had made a recent offer. Their wives had been classmates at Vassar College, attending a Bible study there, and the two couples had become good friends. (The Weyerhausers had sent a large financial gift to support the Robinsons' ministry at the Village Church.) Now Weyerhauser asked Paul to fly Christian college students to remote wheatfields in Oregon and eastern Washington. There, with Paul, the students would teach the Bible, preach the gospel, and offer spiritual salvation to workers removed from church during the long harvest season. Weyerhauser knew how quickly the plane could cover the two hundred miles separating farm areas. He made Paul a generous offer to be pilot and administrator.

"It was missionary flying on the home field," Paul and Lillian recall. They had begun to consider the offer, so when Paul met MBI officials, he disclosed the offer but also his desire to wait until they responded. When the Robinsons returned home, they agreed to ask God for clear direction on an important decision. Paul asked God to give a clear sign. If MBI officials responded by February 21, he would go with the training program. If not, he would not keep his friend David waiting. He would accept the position to direct Weyerhauser's ministry to itinerant workers.

Paul heard nothing from MBI for two weeks. So on the morning of February 21, he sat at his desk drafting his telegram of acceptance to Weyerhauser when the morning mail arrived. Two letters were from Moody, one from Culbertson and one from Crowell. Each man expressed strong interest in the Robinson proposal, and Crowell invited Paul to return to Chicago.

"The Institute is definitely interested in the proposed course of missionary flight instruction," Crowell wrote. "However, as I have already told you, we are unable to have any definite commitment until we are able to have the whole question properly surveyed as to costs, methods, curriculum, etc. Would you be interested in making such a survey as soon as convenient for you?" Crowell was asking Robinson to determine whether a missionary aviation training program was truly feasible in Chicago; then the school would make a final decision.

"So here we were with a firm offer of an aviation ministry with Weyerhauser, contrasted with an invitation to merely do a survey," Paul says. But the choice was easy. "I wanted to see missionary aviation go, so I opted for helping run the survey on missionary aviation training. I gave up the solid job with Weyerhauser for a maybe." He was confident God had given him a clear sign with the arrival of the two letters on February 21.

After he finished the survey and visits to many area airports, the school still could not assure him of an aviation program and thus a job. As the Robinsons waited for MBI officials to decide, "we were just trusting the Lord one day at a time," Lillian says simply. "We knew Moody was the Lord's answer. . . . We said no to Weyerhauser and waited to see what would happen. We didn't worry."

His survey seemed promising. Robinson's report recommended that the school rent space from the airport in Elmhurst, about twenty miles west of the campus. He found the airport's arrangements for fuel and oil sales, liability, and operating agreements favorable, and liked the facilities. In addition, he included cost estimates and details for a ground school, as well as a proposed curriculum. Robinson submitted the survey findings and recommendations and headed back to New York to await word.

Almost three months after submitting his proposal at Founder's Week, Paul Robinson boarded the New York Central in Buffalo for a significant trip to Chicago. Crowell had written, asking him to address the Board of Trustees at their April 24 meeting. Crowell thought Robinson would be the ideal salesman for the program. But the pastor/pilot was no more sure of this crowd than had been the six-year-old boy who had once stood on a church pulpit to address 250 adults.

"Crowell thought I could do a better job of selling than he could. I could by no means agree with him. Why he thought a country preacher from the boonies could come in and sell a dozen high-powered industrial and spir-

itual giants what seemed like a crazy idea of training airplane pilots for missionary work I could hardly imagine.
Nevertheless, I agreed to appear."

Despite his uncertainty, Paul slept well in his Pullman
sleeper during the ten-hour ride to Chicago. In the morning he reviewed his report and then enjoyed the passing
scenery until he arrived at the Chicago station.

That afternoon President Will Houghton introduced
Robinson to the board. Robinson felt comfortable seeing
two friendly faces—he had heard Houghton years earlier
at a summer Bible conference, and knew Crowell from his
school days at MBI. The trustees, cordial and interested in
his background as a pastor, quickly put him at ease. Clearly
they considered him more than "a country preacher from
the boonies." They asked Robinson about specific ways
missionary aviation would help missionaries and mission
agencies. More questions followed, with much discussion.
Robinson answered clearly and told them about the vision
of Christian Airmen's Aviation Fellowship, the first agency
dedicated to preparing and sending pilots to help missionaries and nationals. CAMF was searching for pilots with
good Bible training and unique skills for mission flying. At
this point, they were contacting Air Force and Navy veterans from World War II.

---

*The first school to train missionary pilots
would quickly become the
premier program of its kind.*

When Robinson had answered all their questions, there
was a lull before Trustee Robert W. Nicholas rose from his
chair. "If the rest of you feel as I do, and if this young man
will help us, I feel we should proceed," said the successful

real estate developer of Chicago's west side. "And I should like to have the privilege of buying the first two airplanes for the program."

"That's when I got excited," Paul admits. "I didn't jump off a chair. But I was smiling." And across the room he saw his friend Coleman Crowell grinning. When the meeting ended with a vote approving a pioneer training program for mission pilots, Coleman greeted Robinson with hearty congratulations.

President Houghton welcomed Robinson to the Moody family and asked him to leave that night for the National Association of Evangelicals convention, then underway. Eight hours after arriving in Chicago, Robinson was enroute to Minneapolis to announce MBI's new program in mission aviation.

At the NAE convention, Robinson met with MAF President Jim Truxton and other evangelicals as he discussed the new program. Less than one week later, on May 1, 1946, the flight program lifted off. The first school to train missionary pilots would quickly become the premier program of its kind. But the first classes at Elmhurst Airport would be times of learning to improve and revise an unknown.

MBI placed an order for two Piper Cubs quickly, and Paul flew the first plane back from the Piper Pennsylvania factory on June 6. A strong head wind slowed the plane from its average cruising speed of 75 MPH to only 60 MPH, stretching the flight to eight hours. But events sped up after that.

By fall the program was ready. A dozen students, one flight instructor (Robinson himself), and two Piper airplanes launched the program. Ground school was held on the Chicago campus, and flight lessons took place at Elmhurst. Student pilots completed at least fifty flight hours and then could test for a private license.

At first Paul intended to teach missionaries to fly. However, he soon realized, along with the missions agencies, that fliers should be specialists with mechanical aptitude and technical skills, who could serve general missionaries with transportation and communication. The first students, set on being missionaries, had limited mechanical aptitude and wanted the airplane to be like a utility vehicle, a sort of high-flying jeep.

In 1948 MBI President Houghton called a conference of mission officials to see whether Moody really was helping the agencies with its program. About twenty mission boards, including MAF and JAARS, attended. They asked the urgent questions and then came to a conclusion.

"Do we have a need?" the officials asked. "If we do, let's step up the program to the professional level. Otherwise, let's forget it. We don't want to encourage missionaries to fly when they aren't competent."

The consensus was clear: the mission agencies wanted a larger, more professional flight training program. Thus, Houghton mandated a revamping of the MBI aviation program. Paul liked his orders. He knew that some missionaries had arrived on the field with the minimum fifty hours flying time ill-prepared for the rigors of flying in a remote area.

"We had to decide whether we would be a professional or amateur program. We had two choices: quit or go all the way with a professional maintenance and pilot training school." Moody chose to create a professional program and added several instructors to teach flight and mechanics courses.

Students would need more flying and must earn both private and commercial licenses. "The standard was not licensing but proficiency," Robinson emphasized. "You need at least a commercial license to be a proficient pilot." Students who needed more flying to be proficient would have to take more. The Federal Aviation Agency requirement was now 200 flight hours for a commercial license, but students were soon amassing more than 300 hours in the three-year program.

Robinson added faculty and planes. By 1949 the fleet included a three-seat Piper PA-12, a four-seat Stinson Voyager, and three other planes. Five faculty members led flight and mechanics courses.

Later the planes and hangar identified their owner and their mission: "MBI Missionary Flight Training." Paul Robinson's dream was realized—training men for mission aviation ministry. Following World War II, the country preacher had lost his own missionary flying dream due to age. Now he would lead hundreds of men to fill his place. During the next forty-four years (1947-1990), more than six hundred students would graduate from the flight, avionics, or maintenance specialist programs,[3] most to serve missionaries worldwide.

Notes

1. Kay Oliver, "Paul Robinson: Winging It," *Moody Monthly* (September 1975), p. 123.
2. Robert G. Flood and Jerry B. Jenkins, *Teaching the Word, Reaching the World* (Chicago: Moody, 1985), p. 193.
3. Including students earning certificates in airframe and powerplant, 614 students have been graduated through 1990. (Data from Office of the Director, Moody Aviation, spring 1991.)

8

From Skis to Skies

By 1949 the Moody aviation course was growing rapidly. Three flight instructors and two mechanics instructors helped Robinson teach an increasing number of students. But two developments would spur growth further. Elmhurst Airport was about to close, so Moody Aviation had to find a new home for its planes and flights. Second, Robinson knew he had to observe, first-hand, missionary aviation operations on a foreign field.

Robinson solved this second need first, when W. Cameron Townsend, director of Wycliffe Bible Translators, invited Crowell and Robinson to join him on a trip through Central and South America to see the operation of Jungle Aviation and Radio Service, Wycliffe's new aviation ministry. Their thirty-day trip was an eye-opener, showing Robinson some of the special challenges facing missionary aviators. His journal account, published in *Moody Monthly*, reveals some of the obstacles and joys of early missions flying.[1]

One week after arriving in Mexico City, Crowell and Robinson joined a JAARS pilot at the Tuxtla base for a short flight to a jungle airstrip on the side of a mountain. Minutes later as they prepared to land, the pilot spotted the runway. Paul wrote: "The landing strip is nine hundred feet long and slopes so that there is a ninety-foot drop from one end to the other. We rolled less than a hundred feet after landing. Because of the heavy load, I got out and walked to the top of the airstrip. Even so, it took more than normal cruising power to taxi the plane up the incline.

"The take-off was accomplished, of course, by turning around and taking off downhill. Here again there was no chance to misjudge. Missionary pilots must be well trained."

Six days later, after stops in Panama, Colombia, and Ecuador, including a landing at 10,000 feet in the Andes Mountains, he wrote from Lima, Peru. Enroute to the Wycliffe jungle base in Pucallpa, three hundred miles away, the Moody officials ascended to 14,000 feet in their Grumman Duck, a large but old amphibious plane and Wycliffe's only aircraft. "Once beyond the mountains, we were above jungle. It was almost more breath-taking than the mountains. Jungle and sky and sky and jungle, with not a break anywhere except here and there a river. Pucallpa turns out to be a real jungle town of about 1,000."

Here they visited with Brethren missionary Joe Hocking, working with his wife and six children. That afternoon, "several of us flew over to the site of a new jungle base being erected on a lake about three miles from Pucallpa. Landing on the lake, I practiced a bit of wingman operation. In this amphibian [Duck], when landings are made in rivers with swift currents, the copilot must climb out with a long rope, walk to the tip of the wing, fasten the rope to the wing strut and throw the other end of the rope to someone ashore.

"This is a mighty tricky operation. The slip stream from the propeller blasts you as you climb out over the side, and as you near the wing tip your weight forces the 'float' down into the water so that the river rushes over the top of the lower wing panel, nearly washing your feet out from under you."

The plane was vital in the village of Huau (pronounced "wow"). Robinson accompanied the pilot as he delivered a thousand pounds of supplies, including a radio and a gasoline generator, to three missionary women who ministered to the Piro Indians there. Also aboard were two missionaries who would continue on to No Me Olvides, the next stop up the river. By plane the distance is a short hop, compared to a day by boat. After a Huau supper, one of the three missionaries, linguist Esther Matteson, told the Moody visitors that several Indians were gathering in the small hut for a time of fellowship and song. "Among them were several who had never heard the gospel," Robinson wrote.

"It was thrilling to see how eagerly these people drank in the glorious salvation story, and then see two of them accept Christ as their Savior. Thanks to the ministry of the planes and radio, Esther has not only been able to establish herself in this Indian village, but has been able to remain long enough to learn the Indian language, reduce much of it to writing, and translate portions of the Word of God.[2]

"In less than two years here she has also taught many of the Indians to read and has seen a number of them come to a saving knowledge of Christ. Even so, we were again deeply impressed by the great need for men missionaries."

Just before departure from Quito, Ecuador, he met with MAF President Jim Truxton and MAF pilot Nate

Saint, "from whom we gathered a great deal more valuable information about evangelizing the northern portion of South America—a task which we agreed would be virtually impossible without the use of missionary planes supported by a network of radio communications."

By the time Robinson returned to the United States, he knew his program was moving in the right direction. Still, they needed more room and the ability to conduct ground school at the airport. That was coming soon, in the form of a new airport.

Only months after Robinson returned to Chicago, he learned that the Elmhurst property, with its choice land near two major thoroughfares, had been leased to someone else. The airport would close, and high-tension power lines and road improvements would follow. But Robinson soon found space available at Wood Dale Airport, less than eight miles away. Moody Aviation rented space at the airport for four years, finally buying it in 1954. The school purchased all the shops, tools, hangars, and ninety acres of land, including airstrips.

The all-grass airfields permitted takeoffs and landings in any direction, and flight operations could continue even when the prevailing winds shifted. Planes were grounded only during heavy spring rains. When the rains came, they brought what the students fondly dubbed "Mud Week," when flight schedules were scratched.

A few planes even flew with snow on the ground. Students removed the landing wheels and fastened skis on five planes for several winters in the mid-fifties. "Students enjoyed the novelty of the skis," Robinson says, though their planes were quickly airborne after a short departure run. Still, replacing the wheels with skis was extra work, and the faculty and most students cheered when the flight school finally obtained a dump truck fitted with a snow plow in 1960. A few students, though, bemoaned the loss of their ski patrol. Yet even those students knew their goal was the skies, not skis.

More and more students applied to take the missionary technical course, attracted by the free tuition[3] and MBI's strong reputation in missions. With more applicants to the program, Robinson increased the testing procedures to be sure that the most qualified candidates entered the course and, eventually, the missionary skies. In 1960 students were required to complete a two-year pre-aviation program. They entered the program after completing a series of aptitude tests that measured mechanical and problem-solving skills. Also that year, the school began its annual Flight Camp: part camp, part evaluation, and all excitement. Students completing the pre-aviation curriculum (mostly Bible and general education courses) were invited to the camp for one week of testing, including flight instruction.

Today Moody Aviation has three FRASCA computer-enhanced flight simulators to train students.

Robinson describes the early Flight Camp this way: "A five-day program of severe practical tests, including five thirty-minute periods of individual flight instruction." The setting at Wood Dale, about twenty-five miles from the Chicago campus, made the experience fun yet stressful for the would-be student-pilots. Robinson and his staff also found the week challenging.

"Meals were brought from the Institute and twenty-four mattresses were placed for sleeping. At the end of the five days, the staff and Franklin Broman, MBI dean of men, came together to select twelve recruits for the coming third year class. This was the most difficult task we had to perform. To not make the list was a severe blow to those who were left out, as well as to us as a staff. We often prayed all night before posting the list.

"The twelve students who were accepted for further training had the weekend to find rooms or apartments, and the following Monday, classes, shop, and flight schedules began." For these students, "Flight Camp was over and the aviation phase of training had begun."

The Wood Dale facility seemed to have everything: two heated shops, kitchen and lounge, and room for the ground school, which was held the first few years on the main campus because Elmhurst Airport was too small. Moody Aviation[4] quickly purchased a Link flight simulator; today Moody Aviation has three FRASCA computer-enhanced flight simulators for advanced student training.

Despite the larger facilities, Robinson found himself "amazed how quickly all this space evaporated as we grew and were required to meet additional Federal Aviation Agency demands." FAA regulations required separate rooms for each major phase in airframe and powerplant (A&P), the two main programs of the ground school.

Though Moody Aviation wanted to qualify as an FAA-approved flight school and an A&P school, they lacked the necessary partitioned space. So they requested and received FAA permission to paint stripes on the floor to represent walls, imaginary boundaries for each "room."

When FAA inspectors visited they were impressed by the careful organization. Every tool was in its place, the "rooms" were meticulously clean. Lillian Robinson remembers how that satisfied the guests. "It's safer in the airplane business to have nothing you can stumble over, and they saw we had a clean operation. D. L. Moody was a bug for keeping things clean, so it made sense we should too."

"When the FAA saw our practice and procedures, they gave us understanding," Robinson adds. The yellow stripes created imaginary rooms for such courses as machine shop, welding, sheet metal, hydraulics, and paint and refinishing, until actual walls could be built.

Twelve years after his first visit, Robinson returned to South America to learn about the present needs in missionary aviation and to evaluate his program. He helped then-MAF President Grady Parrott fly a Cessna Skyhawk from Los Angeles to Sao Paulo, Brazil, and then began a revealing tour. Everywhere signs pointed to the growth of mission aviation. There were scores of new mission airstrips. The two men agreed that pilot skills were improving, and as a result, mission airstrips could be more marginal, "and at the same time safe in the hands of the professional pilot," Robinson noted. He marveled as he considered the relatively few major air accidents for the area. "Given the exposure to dangerous conditions in developing areas, it is amazing there are no more accidents."

Parrott discussed a major safety factor: rating pilots according to their skills and experience. New pilots had to spend months after arriving on the field on check rides to satisfy veteran pilots before they received an assignment.

During one five-hour leg across the northern part of the continent, Robinson stared down at solid jungle. During another leg, Parrott and he soared above the mouth of the Amazon River, two hundred miles wide and full of alligators. Robinson thought about how important the plane had become to missionaries in ministry, saving time and bypassing the common dangers of jungle and river travel. Though he could not fly for a mission, he was content knowing God was using him to prepare hundreds of young men to serve many missions agencies.

Robinson returned with a few new ideas for the program but was satisfied overall. Safety would always be the paramount concern: to give a safe, comfortable flight to every passenger, missionary, pastor, or local citizen. Ironically, his concern for safety would eventually force him to abandon Wood Dale Airport. O'Hare was coming, and a national search for a new place for the Moody flight school began.

Chicago's O'Hare International Airport, destined to become the world's busiest, was completed in the early sixties, and Wood Dale was only three miles away. The FAA requirements ensured safety for the time being, but they also stifled flight training. (This was before more sophisticated radio communications and tracking.) Airliners normally approached the airport at eight hundred feet above the ground. As a result, Moody pilots had to fly at three hundred feet, below the O'Hare traffic. And that, Robinson knew, spelled trouble.

"Three hundred feet is too close to the ground for safety. It's true we had a fine relationship with O'Hare, and no near misses. However, that was no place for us, and we began casting around for some place to go." Though it meant relocation, perhaps to another state, Robinson met with MBI administrators, including President William Culbertson, and explained the need. Culbertson agreed and approved the search for a new airport, up to five hundred miles from the Chicago campus, if necessary. The national search had begun.

Robinson requested the five hundred mile radius knowing he might not find the ideal airport in Illinois or even the Midwest. While Wood Dale's grass runways permitted takeoffs in all directions, neither the weather nor locale was ideal for learning mission-flying techniques. The occasional heavy spring/summer thunderstorms and low cloud cover would postpone flights and delay schedules, and the flat Illinois plain did not simulate typical primitive flying conditions. Moody officials had considered paving the airstrips in the early sixties; now, with the completion of O'Hare, Robinson searched for airports that were already paved, were located in rural, less cluttered skies, and featured terrain that could simulate missionary flying conditions.

By the mid-sixties the fleet numbered twenty-two planes, including five all-fabric Pipers with robust names like the Supercruiser and the Vagabond.

Robinson and his Moody colleagues spent five years searching for the right airport. Robinson wrote letters to officials in more than one hundred cities, asking if they were interested in having a flight school at their field. Chief Flight Instructor Dirk Van Dam, A&P Director Bob Rich, and Robinson visited dozens of cities. At several airports they met with city and aviation officials. At others no meetings had been scheduled, so they simply flew reconnaissance: if they liked what they saw, they'd land and ask for an impromptu meeting with an airport official; if the airport looked unacceptable, they just flew on.

Moody Aviation was an attractive prize for a small municipal airport. By the mid-sixties the fleet numbered twenty-two planes, including five all-fabric Pipers with robust names like the Supercruiser and the Vagabond. There were specialty planes, such as the radio-equipped Stinson Voyager and the metal-framed Apache and the Comanche. And there were the common but dependable Cessnas, including five 150s and a 172. Lots of take-offs and landings would mean big business to an airport, and the expertise of the faculty and student pilots would mean that the airport could offer more services to pilots.

The ideal airport had to meet some unusual criteria, however, and the list soon narrowed. "We wanted mountains, we wanted weather," Robinson explained. Both those conditions would be ideal in preparing students for rugged jungle flying, and the search shifted to a small country setting without the big city conveniences. "We wanted weather variety and terrain variety," adds Rich. "Hills, valleys, and water for training with sea planes. We also wanted a community that would help our [faculty] families adjust, with good schools and churches."

Officials from more than ninety cities responded to the school's inquiries, anxious for the business. Eventually a small Tennessee town at the base of the Great Smoky Mountains appealed to Robinson. At first, "Elizabethton wasn't high on our list, but its weather and terrain made it attractive. We would take the haze, fog, thunderstorms— all the weather the Smokies could provide."

Actually, the Elizabethton weather still would prove itself quite favorable, for little snow fell during the winter, and the occasional fog would burn off by midday. And the people were friendly; in fact city officials came to visit Moody Wood Dale before Robinson toured Elizabethton. The officials flew to O'Hare and drove a rental car to Wood Dale to promote their airport. They soon understood one reason Moody Aviation wanted a new setting.

"The field was covered with at least a foot of snow and they could see a part of our problem," Robinson says. "These men had a problem themselves in an airport that was not an asset." They had a beautiful airport that the federal government helped them build after World War II as part of a plan to improve small-town economies in the Southeastern United States. They had an excellent paved runway that met FAA standards but little business.

"Elizabethton had put up a hangar, where several private planes were stored," Robinson recalls, "but the airport basically was unattended. The city found they had acquired more airport than business—an expense that many taxpayers were not happy about." As the two sides talked, Robinson sensed good timing and a good fit. "It became more and more apparent that they had 'happened' along at just the right time."

Moody representatives visited Elizabethton within one month. During a special luncheon with the mayor and other officials, they learned about weather, housing, school, terrain, and beautiful Lake Watauga, a ten-minute flight from the airport and perfect for sea-plane operations.[5] Ten minutes in the opposite direction from the lake was Tri-City Airport, an important airline terminal with instrument approach and landing facilities. Before leaving the pleasant community of 12,000, Moody Aviation officials said they would recommend the facility to MBI leaders upon their return. They boarded their plane pleased also by the distance—Elizabethton was exactly five hundred air-miles from Chicago, meeting President Culbertson's requirements.

MBI officials liked the plan and gave approval. Elizabethton liked the new business possibilities and began to work on an agreement. Moody would build several buildings and divide any profit that would accrue from services it provided nonstudents. In return, the city provided a four thousand foot paved runway and obtained FAA clearance to sell Moody Aviation six acres of property adjacent to the airport. The land would belong to MBI, and the school could still have unlimited access to the airport. The FAA, which usually denied such access, agreed that MBI could use the land to build about 50,000 square feet of structures without the airport's having a legal claim to the land or its buildings.

The two parties unraveled bureaucratic red tape with frequent visits to Nashville, Elizabethton, and Wood Dale, including visits with the Tennessee Office of Education and the governor. Finally, in the fall of 1967, several flight instructors, eight senior students, and Robinson set up school at Elizabethton. Two years later the remaining classes would join them, and the aviation school, consisting of flight, maintenance, and avionics departments, would become an extension campus five hundred miles from Chicago. But as students and staff alike quickly discovered, a welcome awaited them at "Betsy."

Notes

1. "Latin American Diary . . ." *Moody Monthly* (August 1949), pp. 836 ff.
2. Esther completed translation of the gospel of Mark in 1949 and served Wycliffe in Colombia, Bolivia, and other countries over four decades. She received the Alumnus of the Year award from MBI in 1991 and continues to serve as a linguistic consultant to Wycliffe.
3. Students paid only for flight time, which paid for the airplane's operating costs. Today MBI provides each student an annual subsidy of about $10,000. Even so, with rising costs, including insurance and a student's personal set of tools, a student will pay almost $30,000 for his flight school training. See chapter 13 ("Pilots, Male and Female") for more information on costs.
4. Moody Aviation is the common name for the flight program, but the actual name is the Department of Missionary Aviation Technology of Moody Bible Institute. The program's previous names were Department of Missionary Technical Training and, prior to the Baccalaureate degree program in 1966, the Missionary Technical Course.
5. The school operated a float plane through the 1970s, and students learned gliding techniques with a glider on site until the mid-eighties. Both planes have been sold due to cost and minimal use. Today, some of the missions agencies give training on these planes at their home bases.

9

From Betsy to Brazil

Officials from Washington, Chicago, and Nashville shared the platform in April 1970 when the school was formally dedicated. "Welcome to this special day as we dedicate the Moody Aviation school at Elizabethton," Robinson announced. But for the students and staff, all of whom were already at work in Tennessee the previous fall, the community had become simply "Betsy." Friendly, small, a place for dreams, Betsy had opened her arms, offering housing in town, often with local families. Betsy was the final stop in a student-pilot's journey to mission service.

Moody added much to the Elizabethton aviation complex. Its new building covered 64,000 square-feet. A few years later Tennessee Governor Winfield Dunn awarded Moody Aviation's Bob Rich a special maintenance/safety award for developing an "outstanding aviation maintenance training program." The program had grown in stature and impact. That April afternoon more than a thousand attended the dedication, including congressmen and FAA officials. Only a few years earlier an FAA administrator in a *Chicago Tribune* report called the Moody Aviation operation one of "the most comprehensive and exacting training programs anywhere."[1]

The new facility allowed faculty and staff to maintain that reputation. All rooms were divided, including a flight planning and dispatch room, and flight and maintenance classrooms. Another section contained welding, machine shops, and magnaflux. Aircraft and engine overhaul now took place in airframe and powerplant labs, and a fully equipped parts and tools stockroom opened.

The new runway lies between two mountain ranges: the one to the north rises to 4,500 feet; the other, at 6,000 feet, lies due south. Near the approach pattern for landing at the runway's northeast end, a rocky outcropping called Forge Hill rises seven hundred feet above the level of the strip. That adds a little adventure to some landing approaches—nothing serious, but similar to the less-than-routine landings missionary pilots face. The students and staff also developed airstrips on Walnut Mountain and near Watauga Lake that duplicated primitive landings. Watauga Lake also allowed students to practice water landings with a Piper Cub airplane on pontoons.

Everything was in place for Robinson to direct operations at the new site—everything but Robinson, who quietly stepped out of the spotlight. He appointed his chief flight instructor, Dirk Van Dam, as director of Moody Aviation. Van Dam had assisted in finding the new location and was airport manager at Wood Dale. Meanwhile, Robinson chose to return to Chicago to direct admissions to the flight program. Moody Aviation needed someone to coordinate admissions to the pre-aviation program that now was five hundred miles north of Elizabethton. Robinson welcomed the chance to counsel pre-aviation students in Chicago, and he also started the Pre-Aviation Club at MBI. He offered personal counsel, showed pilot candidates films, and scheduled missions speakers and lectures. Most important, he screened applicants to the program, giving aptitude tests and conducting interviews. Meanwhile, his school continued strong at Betsy.

"I had no ambition to become a leader. I wanted to start a work and leave it in the hands of competent people," Paul explained years later, with Lillian at his side. "I was constrained to do this work." Lillian glanced at her husband and added, "Paul had good vision." That vision was obvious as both a pastor and a missionary pioneer. Robinson's vision included seeing the potential in each student. When students at MBI-Chicago worried about Flight Camp or their qualifications, Robinson would encourage them. And once students had graduated from Moody Aviation, Robinson followed their careers. John Miller, a member of the first graduating class from Betsy in 1967, has spent eighteen years with Mission Aviation Fellowship and credits Robinson with rekindling his missionary vision.

Miller intended to investigate MAF shortly after earning his flight instructor rating but began to work as an A&P mechanic instead. Later, a fiberglass manufacturer of industrial and sporting goods hired him as a corporate pilot. He flew executives and sales people around the country in the company twin-engine Cessna 310.

"I fear I was slowly beginning to drift in my commitment to missions. The corporate flying was fun, the boss was talking about getting a jet, and the benefits were certainly good." Then two years after graduation, Miller received a telephone call. It was his friend Paul Robinson, checking up on him.

"John, I don't know what you're doing or where you are, but you've been out of school a couple years. I understand you're not aligned with a mission agency yet. Listen, there are many opportunities with MAF."

Miller recalls how the conversation ended. "Mr. Robinson's familiar, gentle voice is kindly reminding me, 'There's work to be done, son.' I don't have to guess where he got the notion I needed a boot. Mr. and Mrs. Robinson humbly love their Lord and the Spirit directs their lives. So as we say in aviation, I made a slight off-course correction and contacted MAF once again." (The John Miller story appears in chapter 2.)

Robinson interceded for some students and challenged others. "He would consult students without being harsh or dictatorial," says Bob Rich, a faculty member and pre-aviation coordinator with Moody Aviation for thirty-three years. "He was able to take the fellows and sit down with them. He'd talk through the problem and help them put it into perspective. At other times he would meet with a student who was not spiritually motivated or lacked the necessary skills to continue the program. He was the pastor type who could do it. He could lay down the alternatives and then would let the student express himself. Sometimes he'd talk to the faculty, too, if we were putting unfair pressure on the student."

As a former pastor, Robinson enjoyed counseling students on both academic and personal matters. During discussion of classroom issues at the weekly faculty meetings, members sometimes would mention students having problems inside or outside of class and ask for prayer and advice. "Paul knew the students' family life," Rich says. "We were concentrating on the shop and training program, and, with his information, he could counsel us. Sometimes a student was under pressure that we weren't aware of."

Paul takes great pride in "his boys," students he has guided into missionary aviation. They are the legacy of a pilot who could not go to Brazil as a missionary airman because of age. "Years after being told I couldn't go, I remember looking at a picture of ten of our pilots, all serving in Brazil. I thought, *That's where I wanted to go. I didn't get there, but these ten did.* Eventually more than that went to Brazil. Dozens went. I couldn't do it. But my boys did it for me."

He once told a group of friends and supporters that had he gone to Brazil as he wanted, he would have been "just one poor missionary pilot running around in Brazil." Instead "there are now hundreds of missionary pilots all over the world. It's clear God knows what He's doing." Citing Philippians 1:12, he says, "These things have happened to you—and to me—so they may fall out to the furtherance of the gospel."

Paul Duffy estimates that 50 percent of all JAARS pilots are graduates of Moody Aviation.

The legacy of Paul Robinson and Moody Aviation is more than just pilots in Brazil. In the past twenty years, 375 students have graduated from the pilot, avionics (radio and electronics) training, and maintenance specialist programs.[2] Of these alumni, 80 percent have served or are serving MAF, JAARS, or one of forty other mission boards.[3] A dozen other Christian schools produce pilots through their aviation programs, but none sends a majority of its students into missions.

"I've visited our fourteen different programs overseas," says JAARS official Paul Duffy, "and Moody is represented in every one. In spiritual maturity, the Moody graduate has an edge over students from other schools."

Duffy, JAARS's aviation director for seven years and now assistant to the executive director, estimates that 50 percent of all JAARS pilots are graduates of Moody Aviation. The remainder come from other flight schools and the military.

MAF President Max Meyers also describes Moody Aviation as the premier school for producing missionary pilots. Meyers has served MAF thirty years, including ten years as a pilot, and calls the school "critical to our future. . . . Moody has been the most fruitful field of training for Mission Aviation Fellowship. And without a doubt, Moody has also been the best. Moody has set out to produce a [pilot] specifically designed for this work, and it has done it well."

The strong link with MAF and JAARS, the two largest mission aviation agencies, is not accidental. Through the years Robinson maintained contact with both, and the two continue to offer technical advice and recommendations to the Elizabethton faculty regularly, as well as visit the school each year during its missions conference. Robinson "had a strong association with MAF from its beginning, and a close friendship with the people involved," Bob Rich says, "and almost as close with the people from JAARS from its beginning."

Rich, who supervised the MA airframe and power-plant school for fifteen years, describes Robinson, JAARS founder Cameron Townsend, and MAF cofounder Grady Parrott as "the same sort of people—people who have a burning desire for missions and all that involves. They had a particular gift to be applied in that area."

Robinson appreciates but deflects the commendations from JAARS and MAF, saying they simply reflect Moody Aviation's ability to shape a pilot whom missions agencies can use. That, after all, was the sole reason for beginning the school in 1946. But the founder of the first school to train missionary pilots admits that a surprise party from Moody Aviation in 1975, just one week before his retirement, made him realize the impact his role at Moody Aviation had on the lives of his faculty, graduates, and missionary aviation.

Paul and his wife, Lillian, had flown in to witness their final graduation ceremony at Moody Aviation. But after a morning chapel message from MBI Dean of Education Alfred Martin, Robinson found the spotlight on him. In a moving tribute, current students stood up one after another to read commendations from former students. The telegrams from South Africa, Indonesia, and Latin American countries lauded the man and the program. Twenty-two pilots serving mission agencies throughout Latin America, all MA alumni, wrote: "God gave a vision. You made it a reality, and we are missionary airmen today through God's faithfulness through you. May your ongoing ministry provide new opportunities in Christ's service."

MAF President Chuck Bennett, an MA alumnus, wired the agency's gratitude. "Our congratulations and thanks for your unique ministry as a founder and pacesetter for missionary aviation. Thank you even more for your personal friendship, confidence, and encouragement in my own life and in the lives of at least three score of our MAF pilots who are at this point serving Christ even more throughout the world."

Tributes and recollections from graduates in the room continued for forty minutes, and Paul and Lillian soon were wiping wet eyes. The most moving tribute was from the junior class, who sang "O Zion Haste" as a class member read a narrative describing overseas mission work before and after trained missionary pilots took to the skies.

In South America, one mission, one road. The week-long journey to a small village. A short stay, a few evangelistic meetings. Off on the same road. Another village, a few more meetings. "You need what?" More Bibles? Maybe next time. More teachers? I'll try my best." Off again on the same road—another week on that road.

Home at last. What have I done? Three long weeks on the road, three days of meetings. I need more help. If only we had wings.

. . . A need, a man with vision. God's plan, God's provision. A week's travel changed to an hour's flight. Time saved, lives saved. God's Word carried farther and faster.

Paul Robinson, like aviation pioneers Cameron Townsend, Grady Parrott, Jim Truxton, and Betty Greene, carried God's Word farther and faster through mission aviation. On wings of love, the Word of God would advance around the world.

Notes

1. Robert G. Flood and Jerry B. Jenkins, *Teaching the Word, Reaching the World* (Chicago: Moody, 1985), p. 194.
2. Of this total, 339 students completed the pilot program, 14 the avionics program, and 22 the maintenance specialist program. (Figures are from the Office of the Director, Moody Aviation, for the years 1970 to 1990.) Since the program began in 1946, 614 students have completed one of the three programs or earned a certificate in Airframe & Powerplant.
3. Gene Getz and James Vincent, *MBI: The Story of Moody Bible Institute*, rev. ed. (Chicago: Moody, 1986), p. 113; and interview with Ken Simmelink at Moody Aviation, November 28, 1990.

10

School Days

On average, every four minutes a Moody Aviation-trained pilot takes off on a mission of love and mercy.[1] They shuttle food, mail, literature, Bible translation material, and medical supplies. And they ferry important human cargo—national pastors and missionaries to remote villages, men and women to medical clinics for emergency treatment. Soaring above the jagged mountains, the thick jungles, or meandering rivers, the pilots shave days off the travel time. In some cases they bring missionaries and pastors into areas accessible only by air. At least half the world's missionary pilots receive their training at Moody.

Why do so many graduates of Moody Aviation enter missions? According to the current director, Ken Simmelink, the reason is one slip of paper. Each incoming student writes a statement of intent, indicating that his plan is to enter missionary aviation after he completes the program. Each year the student renews that commitment with his signature. That statement coincides with the entire purpose of MBI and its flight school. "Because our program is highly subsidized and because the goals of Moody Bible Institute are to train Christian workers, we screen on that basis," says Simmelink.

"The uniqueness of Moody Aviation is that we screen our students, and if their long-range goals are not missions, we don't accept them into the program. So 100 percent of our students are accepted on the basis of their motivation for missions. I don't know another school that does that."

Ken Simmelink knows missionary aviation and pilot training well. He has been director of Moody Aviation since 1983, when he succeeded Dirk Van Dam, and previously was executive vice president of Mission Aviation Fellowship. He was a pilot in Indonesia for eight years and remains a member of the MAF board of directors. The 80 percent of Moody Aviation alumni who enter missionary aviation exceeds rates for the other dozen Christian colleges with aviation programs.[2]

These schools, Simmelink says, have an important role in aviation. "Putting Christians in the airlines is a noble venture. Most do not have a missionary aviation program as such. They're Christian schools with a liberal arts approach, and that's great. It's just that our focus here is different. I won't say it's better, just different. Moody Bible Institute has an objective of training Christian workers that has filtered down to our aviation program. We are geared to train workers for the Christian profession, and missions is our objective."

At "Betsy," student pilots learn to link their missions heart with skilled hands and mind. Technical proficiency is also important, according to Reid Berry, director of development. "They receive very good training to become technically expert." But they will serve "using nontechnical aspects," Reid adds, since they are primarily missionaries serving as world Christians.

The program has not changed much since Moody Aviation completed its move to Tennessee in 1969. The two-year program expanded to three years in 1980 after greater FAA licensing regulations mandated additions to the curriculum, and the faculty wanted to free students for summer ministry and flight experiences. The extra year also permits students more time to assimilate information. The first year curriculum is entirely on the ground, with courses in airframe (fuselage, wings, and rudder) and powerplant (engines). A&P, as it's commonly called, consists of more than 1,900 hours in the shop, as the student strips engines to understand their workings, learns three kinds of welding procedures, and builds airworthy replacement parts in the machine shop. Regarding the plane's powerplant, the student becomes a trouble-shooter, able to recognize and remedy problems.

The first-year student[3] will buy his own tools and learn to arrange them so that he can take inventory in thirty seconds and spot a missing item. Tools left in a plane, whether a flashlight or screwdriver, can cause chaos in an engine. The student also learns to repair the airframe, from propeller tip to rudder tail. The pilot learns how to handle electrical trouble in his aviation electronics course. He will learn how to rebuild portions of a plane through his sheet metal and welding class.

By the end of the first year, a student will have his A&P certificate and will be well on his way to becoming a mechanic/pilot, a hybrid specialist essential in a field where limited manpower requires a pilot to be a jack-of-all-trades. Indeed, on the mission field "he often has to be his own weather service, navigator, cargo handler, and control tower."[4] He also will be an administrator/politician, as he schedules flights, purchases and charges fuel, and deals with government officials. Many of these skills he will learn at Moody Aviation.

Some students who have their A&P certificate apply to work in the Moody Aviation mechanics shop. If the faculty supervisor believes that their skills are well advanced, they may work part-time evenings, Saturdays, and perhaps during summer vacation and receive a salary. All students work in the shop at least every other week once they receive their A&P certificate to gain extra work experience. Though they receive no pay, they receive valuable training and experience as faculty members supervise and approve their work.

Before he leaves the ground, the student will have his first "flight" in one of three flight simulators. The simulator is ideal for instrument training, that is, learning to read and fly by the cockpit instruments without visibility out the windshield. As costs decrease, Simmelink hopes to add more advanced computer simulators with visuals projected on a "windshield" screen. Such simulators would show students the terrain and the outcomes of their maneuvers.

During his second and third years, the student will log more than three hundred hours in the air, all in single engine planes. After graduation, students will need at least twelve more hours for a multi-engine rating to be certified to fly twin-engine airplanes. The second year student begins his primary training with the Cessna 172 Skyhawk. He will fly the Skyhawk all that year, amassing more than one hundred hours and building experience for his two-week cross-country trip the next year.

During his final semester, the student-pilot will be training for an instrument rating, which permits him to fly when limited visibility requires gauges and radio to reach his destination. The student will have at least 125 hours of cross-country flying before receiving his instrument rating. In his senior year the pilot advances to a heavier airplane, either the Cessna 210 or Beechcraft 36. Then the pilot finally flies the Cessna 185 Skywagon.

The Federal Aviation Administration has recognized the quality of the faculty and leaders by designating five Moody Aviation staffers as FAA examiners. Ed Wheeler, MA supervisor of maintenance training, is the FAA examiner in airframe and powerplant for eastern Tennessee and conducts oral examinations of all candidates, including Moody students. Reid Berry, MA director of development, administers flight exams for multi-engine ratings and instrument ratings. In addition, Berry tests and approves flight instructors for eastern Tennessee. Senior flight instructor Ron Royce conducts flight exams to evaluate pilots for private, instrument, and multi-engine ratings.

The chief FAA inspector announced, "From my observation this is the best aviation training school in the nation."

MA Director Simmelink is himself an airman certification representative; his signature upon completion of the three-year flight school authorizes a private pilot's license from the FAA. The secretary to the director, Mary Lee McBee, is a designated written examiner, and conducts all written examinations.

FAA inspectors visit Moody Aviation periodically to evaluate its programs and personnel. During a recent visit, the FAA evaluation team spent three days observing the program and interviewing staff and students. At the conclusion, the four-member team met with MA management and gave their critique. They summarized their findings of the three-day inspection and recertified the school. Then the chief inspector turned to Simmelink and announced, "Ken, I don't have to tell you this, but from my observation this is the best aviation training school in the nation, including the military."[5]

Elizabethton officials have shown their confidence in the MA staff by having MA manage the airport since 1975. Dirk Van Dam served as the first airport manager; since 1983 Reid Berry has been airport manager, the appointee of Simmelink. Though the Elizabethton Airport Commission oversees the entire airport, Berry is on-site to give expert direction and answer questions or complaints from local residents. The line supervisor, who oversees fueling and parking of planes, is a non-MA employee.

Twenty-two faculty teach courses in aviation maintenance, avionics, or give flight instruction. All have at least ten years of experience, and several are former aviation missionaries. Chief flight instructor Bill Powell served eight years in the Philippines and is on service leave with JAARS, still an active member. Flight instructor Ed Robinson has served with MAF thirteen years in Irian Jaya and the Philippines. In addition, missions agencies loan several missionary pilots to MA each year as full-time instructors. These instructors bring new accounts of ministry that encourage students and give would-be pilots practical suggestions and cautions about missionary aviation. They also give helpful background about their own mission agencies.

Ed Robinson resisted mission aviation during his college years, and his struggle reflects two stereotypes about missionary fliers: they're merely glorified bus drivers, not missionaries; and their journeys into Third World villages have lesser impact than big-city missions. His negative attitude might seem surprising, as his father is missionary aviation pioneer Paul Robinson. But his father respected Ed's struggles and did not push Ed to be a missionary pilot. Still Ed decided to attend MBI, and during the first year he realized "missions was for me." But he wanted to have an impact—"to be strategic," as Ed says—and questioned the worth of mission aviation.

"I did mental gymnastics. *There are millions in the cities. These people represent a fraction of the world. I don't want to reach seventy members of a tribe. Let's be strategic.*" So Ed Robinson went to Michigan State University to study political science, then continued to seminary for a degree so that he could teach. But at Trinity Evangelical Divinity School (TEDS), he realized "I'm a doer, not a reader. They looked at thirty journals a month. I love to work with my hands."

During his second year at TEDS, he returned to his apartment after a major thunderstorm dumped fourteen inches of rainfall and found his thesis research awash: all the notes with his blue fountain pen had smeared and run.

But Ed's reaction was gratitude. "I didn't cry. I felt liberated. Later my dad said, 'Hey Ed, why don't you come to flight camp to take a closer look and see if mission aviation is for you.' At age twenty-five, I listened. I told him what my attitude was, that I wanted to be strategic. But I agreed I needed to be current." Like his father, Ed liked planes and flying.

Ed excelled at Flight Camp and, later, in training at Moody Aviation found that he "enjoyed the maintenance and the flying." He began to understand the ministry of mission aviation. "Flying in remote areas wasn't unimportant. We are helping people from every tribe. It's not strategic in numbers, but in terms of what needs to be done before the return of Christ, and in terms of God's love, their needs are great. I felt I could be part of the solution."

Ed and his wife, Nancy, enjoyed their terms in the islands of the Philippines and Indonesia and returned to the United States in 1983 for assistance for their son's learning disability. He's been with MA since. He would like to return to the field now that his son has completed high school, but "I have to decide whether this ministry is better than ministry overseas. In a way I fear sitting before the Lord," he admits. "I may be more effective here than overseas. I can't be more effective as a pilot many more years," says the fifty-year-old Robinson.

Meanwhile, Robinson teaches students many of the lessons he's learned in overseas flying, including how to fly safely and make your passengers feel comfortable. He tells his students about three missionaries he transported at different times who had become fearful of flying because other pilots did not show concern and caution during their trips. When the missionaries boarded his craft, they had taken motion sickness pills or had upset stomachs. One warned him, "Please don't tip the wings."

Students observe in their instructors compassion for missionaries and themselves, and take heart.

Ed has aborted flights because of rough weather and hesitates to fly if he cannot give the passenger a comfortable flight. "It could destroy the passenger's peace and confidence." In mission flying, the passengers always come first, he tells students. That means no rapid descents or steep turns. Missionaries who get white knuckles will be less effective on the ground. "It affects their ability to minister," Robinson says simply.

Students observe in their instructors compassion for missionaries and themselves, and take heart. Teachers demonstrate their deep vision for mission aviation in their very actions, says John Miller, MAF chief pilot in Irian Jaya. The 1967 alumnus remembers being with several other students in a Moody Aviation hangar during a walk-around inspection of an airplane. Flight instructor Ron Royce was explaining the features of the plane and some components the pilot must watch for.

"I really want you guys to learn this. It may save your life someday. It's important."

One student muttered, "Boy, I wish all instructors felt that way."

"What did you say?" Ron asked, unable to understand the student's muttering.

"Oh, no, forget about it. It's nothing."

"No, what did you say? If you have something, let's hear it. I want to know."

"Well, if you really want to know . . ." the student began, and he repeated his statement.

Instead of becoming upset, Royce began to cry. Tears rolled down his face, and with an intense, yet measured voice, he said, "Man, I've dedicated my *life* to this. I'm here to help you. I'm committed to this."

Royce turned around and walked out of the hangar. The students looked down on the ground, some embarrassed and many moved by the man's passion for students and aviation. "We were impressed by what a dedicated individual he was," John says. "I've never forgotten that scene."

Royce has been an MA flight instructor more than twenty-five years, and recently he conducted a chief pilot seminar at MAF headquarters that Miller attended. "He brought all his experiences and humor into the presentation. I don't know anyone quite like Ron as a communicator. He's a tremendous role model and an example to the rest of us."

Miller says Royce remains humble and dedicated to his ministry as a teacher. "I've been around many aviators—military and airline, nonmissions and missions, and Ron is in a class by himself." Royce, Robinson, and Powell are among a much honored, highly experienced faculty that make school days at Moody Aviation both a great education and an inspiration for students who are on their way to a life of ministry on overseas missions fields.

Notes

1. Robert G. Flood and Jerry B. Jenkins, *Teaching the Word, Reaching the World* (Chicago: Moody, 1985), p. 189.
2. Only two other schools, Piedmont Bible College and Grand Rapids School of Bible and Music, have aviation programs designed to train missionary pilots. Key schools contributing missionary pilots through their flight schools are Le Tourneau College and Trinity Western (in British Columbia, Canada). Other schools include Bob Jones University, Calvary Bible College, Heston College, and Liberty University.
3. A first-year student in the program is officially classified as a third-year student, since most students have had two years of college elsewhere to complete their general education requirements. However, some students come to Elizabethton having already completed undergraduate training with a four-year education; therefore, "first-year students" refers to those enrolled in the first-year curriculum at Moody Aviation.
4. Flood and Jenkins, *Teaching the Word*, p. 190.
5. Interview with Ken Simmelink, Moody Aviation, November 28, 1990. The inspection took place in 1987. Simmelink added, "[His statement] was verbal. I don't have a document. But I heard it and my staff heard it."

11

Flying the Friendly Skies

Missionary aircraft have changed since the days of Betty Greene and Nate Saint. Gone are the 1,000 horsepower Grumman Duck and the fabric-covered planes. In their place are sleek, efficient Cessnas with aluminum coverings, turbo-charged engines, and even a few helicopters. Safety features such as Saint's auxiliary fuel supply are now standard, and newer safety innovations such as energy absorbing seats have been added. Still, the world's skies can throw tricks the way of mission aviators.

Pilots often fly over the mountains or jungles of Third World countries, and landings in these regions—or even in pristine valleys where a short airstrip slopes upward—pose challenges. Severe weather, including thunderstorms, fog, and dust storms, can invade an area quickly, and the pilot will not always have advance notice from radar or other tracking systems. A well-trained pilot can tackle these challenges with knowledge and growing skill. The knowledge begins at flight school; the skill comes through specialized training with the pilot's particular agency, followed by on-site training and experience in the country.

At Moody Aviation, students take their first steps toward missionary careers and toward making the vast skies a safe workplace for their ministries. During their final two years as students, they fly three increasingly complex planes, the Cessna 172, 210, and 185. The 172 is the primary trainer. "Our pilots can learn the basics of how to fly in those planes and then transition into the heavier airplanes," says flight instructor Ron Royce. "The 172s also are cheaper to operate than the heavier craft."

The "heavier" aircraft not only weigh more, they require advanced skills. In addition to the wing flaps common to the 172, the 210 has a retractable landing gear and controllable pitch propeller, making them "complex" airplanes as defined by the Federal Aviation Agency. The 185 is almost a fully complex craft, lacking only the retracting landing gear. However, both the 185 and 210 (and its close cousin the 206) are ideal for short runways; the controllable pitch propeller can be turned to angles for takeoffs and landings on a minimum of runway.

Among planes used in mission aviation, the Cessna 185 has been the workhorse, but the 206 is catching up. MAF and JAARS both have about the same number of 185s and 206s. But as they retire the 185s, the agencies replace them with the larger (six seats) 206. Eighty of the planes at MAF are Cessna 185s and 206s, with the larger 206 accounting for more than half. MAF operates only two twin-engine planes, down from eight several years ago. In Indonesia, MAF flies twenty-six craft, and eighteen (69 percent) are either 206s or 185s.[1]

The Cessna 210, the aircraft flown at Moody Aviation, is "not exactly like the 206" but similar, says Royce. He attributes the 206's growing popularity to four factors:

more space, better field of vision, greater cargo space, and easier takeoffs and landings. The greater cockpit space means passengers are not squeezed shoulder to shoulder, and larger doors mean the plane handles cargo more easily than does the 185.

And what about the twin-engine airplane? Though faster and larger, it is not as efficient as the single-engine that dominates mission aviation. A twin-engine burns more fuel, needs a longer airstrip for takeoffs and landings, and must be overhauled more often than a single-engine plane. Like most mission agencies, MAF serves remote, often dirt, airstrips. Pilots need to make frequent trips to bring supplies, medical aid, and the gospel to the back country. A small airplane will do that more easily than a bigger twin-engine plane.[2]

During the 1980s, agencies turned to turbo prop airplanes. Turbos "can carry a large load quickly, and are ideal for famine relief," says Moody Aviation's Reid Berry. "If you have one hundred train car-loads of corn to move into a famine area, you take a big airplane."[3] In certain areas the Cessna 208 Caravan, which has a single-engine turbine jet engine, is replacing the twin engines. It can carry a much larger load than the 185, and it uses readily available (and sometimes cheaper) jet fuel.

With terrain and conditions at Elizabethton similar to those in remote regions where missionary pilots fly, Moody Aviation offers its students practical training. The student pilots will fly into diverse settings during several long-distance trips in their final year. The third year students will take a few trips north into the mountains, extending up to five hundred miles from their Elizabethton base. The major event, however, is the annual cross-country flight. Each fall, seniors fly more than 4,500 miles in a round-trip excursion to California that is anything but a vacation. While enroute, changing weather conditions can force the pilots to change course or file new flight plans with local airports, and mechanical problems will make them perform repairs "on the road."

Though they will fly through the Rocky Mountains, there is little time to admire the scenery. "We fly into the mountains where we have high-altitude strips, and this has a big, adverse effect on the performance of the airplane," says Chief Flight Instructor Bill Powell. "An instructor can talk about it here at sea level, but when the pilots get up about 8,000 feet, they can really see the difference."

The pilot's midpoint is Redlands, California, where he, fellow students, and instructors receive a tour of Mission Aviation Fellowship headquarters. Then they begin their trek back to Tennessee, each of the planes typically carrying two busy students and a watchful flight instructor.

"Forced landing"
is the technical, unemotional term
for a sometimes unsettling,
always unexpected development.

Students continue to become safety conscious during this year by entering practice scenarios. One instructor tells a senior: "A pilot plans to leave Elizabethton on a course for Nashville and has received a threatening weather forecast. A line of thunderstorms lie in his path. What would you do?"[4]

The pilot must make several decisions, including the most basic: Should he even take off? Then the instructor poses other complications enroute on the hypothetical flight, forcing the student to make more decisions. After the decision-making, instructors can ask students for explanations. One student pilot, for instance, decided he would fly despite threatening weather because his passenger needed to reach a meeting. Asked why he chose to fly in dangerous weather, the student explained, "The boss needed to get to Nashville."

"That's not a good reason," the instructor said. "That's peer pressure. Are there additional reasons?"

Teachers ask the students, "Why?" again and again during scenarios. The student must evaluate the reasoning of the pilot, telling what should have been done and whether the decision was poor.

Moody's emphasis on decision-making training is where it should be, according to mission aviation officials. At least 80 percent of flight failures in general aviation come from human factors, and the record at Jungle Aviation and Radio Service is similar, according to JAARS safety director Hank Cook. MAF safety director Bill Born says MAF has a similar record.

"When we look up and see the eagle and how well he flies, man really is out of his environment when he is flying," Born says. "We have to constantly work diligently at that environmental safety." Often those environmental factors will yield only aborted takeoffs, but sometimes there are forced landings.

"Forced landing" is the technical, unemotional term for a sometimes unsettling, always unexpected development—an unscheduled landing in a safe place. The engine may fail, or the pilot may choose to shut down the engine because of a warning light or gauge on the instrument panel, vibration, loss of fuel, or several other possibilities.

The causes of forced landings vary. Bill Powell served eight years in the Philippines before joining the Moody faculty. Still a member of JAARS on indefinite service leave, he remembers once when a fuel pump failed. Another time "an engine decided to destroy itself. A cylinder broke loose from the crankcase, and a piston and rod were beating around. Finally they threw pieces out the side of the cowling. Those things happen occasionally. They happen in the States." He was able to glide the plane safely to a landing.

In the tropics, where temperatures can change wildly in one day, pilots watch closely for fuel contamination. Aviation fuel stays in fifty-five gallon drums, where water contamination is always a threat. If the drums are not stored on their side at a steady pressure, or the temperature varies, moisture from condensation can seep in. And if water collects on the top of the drum, and the temperature drops, the drum can suck moisture through the seal. Meanwhile, over time rust can form inside the drum. "We battle rust all the time," Powell says.

The JAARS veteran has had to abort two flights. Both times fuel contamination was the culprit. In Bagabag near a Wycliffe translation center in northern Philippines, keeping the fuel clean was "a constant battle," Powell recalls. Planes have a filtration system but, even so, mishaps occur. In the first forced landing, he suspects the fuel cap was left off while someone was painting a plane, and a piece of string fell into the line.

"We finally found the string in the filter. It had blocked the fuel flow during takeoff. We were able to clear it out without serious problems and later take off." Another time Powell aborted a takeoff when a piece of rubber obstructed a fuel line. "It probably dislodged from a hose in the fueling system," he says.

Christian aviation agencies have improved safety over the decades with shifting emphases, according to MAF's Bill Born. He says the sixties emphasized better training; the seventies focused on making the plane safer through improvements; and the eighties concentrated on safety management. "So you have a training decade, a decade improving the equipment . . . and then a decade managing safety. The nineties will focus on decision making, or judgment." JAARS's Hank Cook agrees. He believes a pilot's safety increased greatly in the 1970s, when agencies began installing S-frame safety seats in the cockpit.

JAARS led the development of a better seat after Paul Duffy, a JAARS pilot in Ecuador, suffered severe back injuries during a crash landing. The S-frame absorbs much of the vertical energy of a crash. The seat's ability to compress cushions the pilot from the intense physical forces. Duffy, an aeronautical engineer, supervised testing at NASA, with funding and help from MAF and other missions agencies.[5] Already JAARS, MAF, and others have installed S-frame seats in some of their craft. JAARS has permission to use the design in its own aircraft and has placed the seat in most of them.[6]

Two features enhance the seat's safety. The seat cushions are made of Temperfoam®, a dense, impact-absorbing foam originally used in astronaut couches. Recently JAARS has started to use Sunmate® foam, similar to Temperfoam but less sensitive to temperature changes and more fire-retardant. In addition, the rear leg tubes supporting the seat angle backwards, while the S-shaped leg tubes are at the front. "This causes the seat to move rearward, away from the instrument panel, as it collapses in a crash."[7]

Cook agrees that the nineties will be when agencies emphasize developing good judgment, allowing the pilot to "improve his decision-making skills. We won't get away from the skills and the knowledge that pilots have to bring to their trade."

"We emphasize decision making," echoes Moody Aviation's Powell. "The safety record of any pilot is probably due to his ability in this area. His safety record does not depend primarily on his skill in landing on a short airstrip or being able to maneuver below the higher terrain. Safety depends on the pilot's ability to make decisions at the right time."

The faculty at Moody Aviation helps students learn good judgment throughout the pilots' years at the school, though in the final year students receive more intensive training for special skills. They learn techniques for short take-offs and landings, flying low across terrain, and gliding in on a dead-stick landing. Later, when the pilot joins a mission team and serves in a particular field, he will practice and develop his skills with specific airstrips.

Safety is what every missions pilot is after.

The school tries to prepare pilots to recognize their limitations. "If we train a pilot to know his limits—when to turn around, when not to tackle a given airstrip—we have a safe pilot," Powell says. A "hot shot" pilot may handle most situations very well, he says, and soon that pilot feels comfortable and confident. Perhaps too confident. That individual "is being set up for an accident someday." He will meet the challenge he cannot handle. In contrast, Powell says, the student who knows he's not the greatest pilot and is willing to say "no" to certain situations will be safe in the long haul.

What makes a good pilot? Someone who is willing to ask questions—play the role of the skeptic—according to Chief Flight Instructor Powell. And someone who realizes he can always learn something new. "The pilot should always be skeptical, asking questions. 'What if I get up here and can't land? What is my out?' He needs to be suspicious. That pilot should be safe over the long term."

Safety is what every missions pilot is after. And with special presentations and training during candidate orientations[8] and refresher courses during their furloughs, the pilots have contributed to an amazing safety record at the two largest missions agencies. MAF's safety record has eclipsed that of U.S. general aviation, even though MAF pilots fly in more remote areas, often landing on unimproved runways, whereas U.S. private pilots typically land on what the Federal Aviation Agency classifies as "desirable" runways. In the four years from 1986 to 1989, MAF averaged five accidents per 100,000 flight hours, 38 percent less than the average for general aviation (eight per 100,000 hours).[9]

At JAARS, accident rates decreased dramatically after the safety department formed in 1974. During 1987 to 1990, accidents averaged only two a year, with only one accident in 1987 and 1989.[10] Similarly, MAF has averaged only two accidents per year from 1986-1989. Meanwhile, JAARS has had only one fatal accident in forty-five years of flying.

Mission officials attribute their safety record to the strong emphasis on sound judgment, especially the use of the risk/benefit factor. Pilots must ask if the risks of a proposed flight outweigh the benefits. The principle is like a motorist in a hurry to get to work, Born explains. "Stay at the current speed and you may be a little late. Drive faster and you may arrive on time—but you also can be pulled over by a highway patrolman. As the officer writes your traffic ticket, you realize you will arrive much later than you would have by driving at the posted limit. The question the driver should have asked before he hit the gas pedal was, 'Is speeding for the possible benefit of getting to my destination on time worth the risk of being stopped by an officer and getting there much later—plus the fine?'

"We've been teaching the pilots to look at the long-range perspective of what happens if something goes wrong." The answers are easy to see—and costly too: "loss of the aircraft's use, the potential loss of life, the loss of the equipment itself," Born says. "It's vital not to get near-sighted about this one benefit if it's going to shut you down for a year or two."

Weighing the risk/benefit factor occurs most often during threatening weather conditions. "Weigh the benefit carefully," Cook explains. "If you plan to press on and the weather is marginal, what will you gain if you have an accident? You will not gain anything. Tomorrow is another day.

"Sometimes safety seems to hurt efficiency, keeping planes on the ground when missionaries, pastors, and nationals need them. And when a medical emergency beckons, it's hard for a pilot to delay his flight. But waiting may be the safer choice. It's also a time when pilots may see God in action, granting wisdom and sometimes interceding."

Consider Josue Balderas, the MAF pilot serving in Oaxaca, Mexico. (His story is in chapter 1.) Recently he saw God's direction after a delayed medical flight. Medical emergencies form a vital part of MAF ministry, and Josue must be ready to respond quickly, yet safely. He remembers one expectant mother in extended labor, unable to deliver her baby. Problem pregnancies requiring emergency care are fairly common in Oaxaca, according to Josue, but this call surprised him.

"We have a woman who has been in labor four days and needs hospital care," said the radio voice from a distant village. He explained the woman had begun to deliver a breech baby (bottom first). Only the child's hand was showing.

"I'm used to them calling us, saying, 'You have to come out or else she will die.' But the villagers contacted our people three days after they realized they could do nothing," Josue recalls. Unfortunately, strong crosswinds made landing near the patient's village dangerous. After hearing the radio report, Josue chose to delay the flight one day. "I told her family and friends that I wanted to help. But I could not go. The wind was too strong to land." The next morning Josue took off, hoping the winds would abate. During the 35 minute flight, however, gusting winds continued at the airstrip and made a landing impossible. Finally Josue radioed that he would land the Cessna in another area to wait out the winds. But as he came close to the strip, the winds died.

---

*"At MAF we are beyond the
hero syndrome, the feeling that
we can do everything."*

"The villagers were applauding. They knew I intended to fly by, and suddenly they watched as I landed."

Medical personnel moved the woman, and Balderas left quickly. Minutes later he received a radio transmission that the winds had returned.

"That was another confirmation that God was helping. 'Lord, thank you,' I said."

Doctors delivered a dead baby, but they were able to save the mother. Later, the doctors met with pilot Balderas. "The mother would have died minutes later. Thanks for bringing her."

"That type of emergency has happened several times," Josue says. The pressures to fly in immediately are severe, Josue admits, but he often will pray and wait. "Every pilot must decide how far to go in service. I think at MAF we are beyond the hero syndrome, the feeling that we can do everything, that we can pray and then fly in regardless of the dangers. In MAF we will not do that. But we face that pressure in turning down emergency flight requests."

157

During an emergency call to transport patients, "the biggest challenge is knowing the difference between a flight being *needed* and a flight being *safe*," Josue says. "It's a very fine line. We at MAF have concluded that no service is so important that it compromises safety. If it's not safe, the service is not worth it."

Josue knows that saving physical lives is ministry, and often brings a greater openness to the gospel. For all mission pilots, safety means an opportunity to eventually offer a greater, everlasting salvation—the saving of spiritual lives for God's kingdom.

Notes

1. Interview with John Fairweather, MAF technical director, February 15, 1991; and MAF/USA 1991 records.
2. Interview with John Fairweather.
3. Interview with Reid Berry, Moody Aviation director of development, November 26, 1990.
4. A scenario described by Bill Powell during an interview on November 26, 1990.
5. Interview with Hank Cook, JAARS director of safety, May 6, 1991.
6. Andrew B. Douglas, "Safer Seats Offer Hope for GA Fleet," *Aviation Safety* 9, no. 1 (January 1, 1989), pp. 4-5.
7. Ibid., p. 4.
8. During a three-month orientation for new mission pilots, JAARS devotes seven lectures exclusively to safety issues. Topics include procedures, policies, operations manual standards, handling stress, and flights into insecure areas. In addition, instructors in flight and maintenance classes discuss safety elements throughout their courses. MAF spends up to two weeks of its orientation on safety matters.
9. "MAF Safety History, 1964-1989," a chart supplied by Mission Aviation Fellowship, department of operations.
10. "SIL Aviation—Mishaps/Flying Hours," chart prepared by safety department of JAARS. Jungle Aviation and Radio Service is also known as SIL-Aviation, because JAARS is a department of the Summer Institute of Linguistics (SIL).

12

The Maiden Flight

Student pilot Dan Morgan finishes twenty minutes of pre-flight preparations, inspecting wing flaps and ailerons, rudder wires, fuel in lines, landing gear, and various other areas. He tugs here, pushes there, and turns occasionally to his flight instructor, Ron Royce, with a comment or a question. Satisfied, the Moody Aviation senior climbs into the Cessna 185 Skywagon and picks up a clipboard for the final cockpit check. He's almost ready for his maiden flight in a craft more complex than the Cessna 172 he flew last year.

The 185 differs from that aircraft in several ways— different landing gear configuration, heavier weight, more horsepower, and different responses. As Dan settles into the pilot's seat, the first difference he notices is straight ahead, out the window. Unlike the previous plane, the 185 Skywagon offers little forward visibility while on the ground. The Skywagon's nose points upward at about a 15 degree angle, and the pilot will see more sky than horizon while taxiing the plane. During the landing, he must attain that 15 degree attitude for a proper touchdown. The 185's "conventional" landing gear creates this problem. Whereas many planes have one wheel up front and two beneath the wings, the 185 reverses the pattern, with two wheels under the wing and one far back, below the rudder. This configuration is affectionately known as a "tail dragger."

Cleared for takeoff, Dan applies full throttle, the RPMs build, and the Skywagon roars down the runway. As he lifts off, Dan passes the Elizabethton Municipal Airport on his right and the Moody Aviation school on his left. The blue Tennessee skies greet Dan and his instructor as they begin their climb to 8,500 feet over the green and brown hills and lower mountains of Appalachia.

As the Skywagon climbs through the clear November sky, Instructor Royce has Dan begin a series of climbing turns. At cruise climb airspeed, he calls for a 90 degree turn to the right, while maintaining 10 degrees of bank. Later he requests a 180 degree turn to the left, using a 20 degree angle of bank. He repeats the request in Spanish: "Cientoochenta grados a la izquerda con viente grados de banquero."

"De Acquerdo (I agree)," Dan replies.

Royce gave the instruction in Spanish "to break the tension," he says later, but it is a reminder that most missionary pilots will need to become bilingual before they are ready to work with the nationals. Dan spent part of one summer in Honduras with more than a dozen other students, installing a water system. He returned conversant in Spanish and confident of his missions commitment. "I wanted to be sure I wouldn't get out to the mission field and then bow out," he explains of his adventure while a student at Wheaton College, Illinois.

During fifteen days in a village, Dan and his class-mates gave testimonies, sang, and sometimes brought the gospel message. "When we were done there were fifteen believers. Before then, there hadn't been any in the village. It was an enormous confirmation that mission work is val-id. God was saying to me that mission work was a good way to reach people. He was saying, 'I'll bless your efforts, es-pecially if you're doing it for My glory.' I returned fired up about missions, and over time, about missionary aviation."

And so Dan is airborne at 7,800 feet, listening to in-structor Ron Royce give directions as he learns to fly a new aircraft. Ron asks for a full 360 degree turn to the right at a sharp 30 degree bank. The wing flaps are partially extend-ed as Dan proceeds at the "best angle of climb" airspeed. The hills and valleys pirouette below as Dan turns the Skywagon in the empty practice skies of Tennessee's Tri-Cities area. The engine's motor drones on faithfully .

Royce commends Dan after the pilot levels off after one turn. "You leveled nicely. Most guys tend to continue the climb because they aren't aware of what the level flight attitude [position] looks like." Dan continues to the 8,500 altitude and levels the plane for cruising. When the se-quence of climbing turns started at 2,000 feet the fuel/air mixture was set for 19 gallons per hour (GPH). As the climb progressed into thinner and thinner air, Dan slowly reduced the fuel mix, "leaning" the mixture to maintain the proper fuel-air mixture. Thus he arrived at 8,500 feet with the gauge at 16 GPH. Once at cruise configuration, Dan could reduce the power setting even more to econo-mize on fuel. He decreases the fuel flow gradually, finally stabilizing at 12.7 GPH.

Dan has little time to enjoy the Appalachian scenery. Besides, he'd seen it often during the past year as he flew the other two planes into the designated practice area. Even if Dan could enjoy the view, he'd probably vote it only second to his lovely hometown in Colorado. Dan grew up on a ranch thirty miles north of Colorado Springs, where Pike's Peak dominates the skyline, often wearing its snow-white cap into July. Tending horses and chickens were fun chores for Dan, his two brothers, and one sister.

Dan received Jesus Christ as a child and became interested in missionary aviation one summer while helping as a cook at Lost Valley Ranch in the Pikes Peak region west of Colorado Springs. He worked with Kevin Heassler, who told him about Moody Aviation, where Kevin was enrolled. Dan later contacted the school and, after completing general education requirements at Wheaton College, was accepted for flight training.

Mission pilots want and make no profit in their service for Christ and His kingdom.

Cruising at 8,500 feet, Dan is getting ready for a series of stalls and near-stalls that will show him the handling characteristics and abilities of the Skywagon when pushed to the limit. The Skywagon has been aloft about forty minutes, and Royce turns slightly to the student and talks to him through their headsets.

"We're more than halfway though this lesson. Are you tired yet?"

"No," Dan answers simply.

"Oh, that's too bad. I brought some Coke and peanuts with me," Royce quips.

Throughout the flight, Royce asks the pilot questions, ranging from the technical to the practical. After a couple of turns, Royce asks, "In steeper and steeper turns, you're going to lose some airspeed. Is that right?"

"Yeah," Dan replies with confidence, reminded of a basic principle he learned much earlier, but one always to keep in mind. Later, the instructor asks Dan to explain the difference between private and commercial aviation. Only pilots with a commercial license can fly passengers for hire. It's an important distinction, as mission pilots fly as private pilots almost exclusively; they want and make no profit in their service for Christ and His kingdom.

When it's time to practice stalls, Royce asks Dan to adjust the flaps, airspeed, and other settings to simulate four basic configurations: take-off, departure, approach, and landing. Dan performs two stalls in the landing configuration. With full flaps and airspeed at 65 knots, Dan pulls the 185 nose up, approaching an intentional stall. A buzzer warns of the impending crisis, and Dan feels the stall sensation as the wings begin to lose lift. The nose levels and then dips—the Skywagon has stalled. Dan recovers by increasing power, adding airspeed, and retracting the flaps when speed permits. The plane soon regains the proper attitude (position in space). A short time later Royce asks Dan to repeat the stall using a slightly different recovery technique. This time Dan retracts the flaps more slowly, and the plane gently recovers.

"Good. That's much smoother, isn't it?" Royce asks. Dan agrees.

In a stall, the plane's wing basically stops developing lift. Stalls can occur at any speed, altitude, or attitude. Dan practices imminent stalls: the stall warner sounds, and just as the plane hesitates, beginning its stall, Dan adds power. While simulating a stall occurring shortly after takeoff, Dan enters a climb while rolling into a turn. The stall warner sounds, and Dan increases power and gradually retracts the flaps. He presses the rudder pedals to counteract torque and keep the plane in a coordinated turn.

Royce draws Dan's attention to the temperature gauge after some stalls and while cruising at slow speeds. "In takeoff and departure stalls, it's common to see the engine temperature increase," Royce later tells an observer along for the ride. "I wanted to develop Dan's sensitivity to the cylinder head temperature and to have him monitor it during stalls and recovery from stalls. The same goes for slow flying."

The temperature gauge has a red line for a clear visual warning to pilots as they monitor the instrument. The pilot needs to know that he can reduce the engine temperature four ways: decrease the power, enrich the fuel mixture, open the cowl flaps, or increase the airspeed. Before starting the stalls, Royce had Dan enrich the mixture (increasing the fuel flow) and put the cowl flaps in the open position.

Dan Morgan and Ron Royce head back to the Elizabethon airport, satisfied with his maiden voyage, and now prepare for the landing in this tail-dragger. As they maneuver toward their final approach, Ron spots a Beechcraft ahead of them, glistening in the late morning sun. It's four miles from the landing strip, and perhaps two miles in front of them when Ron hears a radio transmission from his good friend Franklin Graham, who's returning to the Moody Aviation hangar to pick up his twin engine Beechcraft Baron BE58-P. Graham, president of Samaritan's Purse, a Christian relief agency in nearby Boone, North Carolina, flies the Baron to Moody ten to twelve times each year for maintenance at the Moody shop. His is one of dozens of aircraft serviced annually by student mechanics and professional supervisors at the FAA-certified repair station.

Graham's approach from the east brings him swooping down across a nearby mountain, and the two pilots begin a friendly banter. "You say you're one mile out? Looks more like four to me!" Royce declares.

"That's what we call a country mile," Graham replies, his southern drawl thick and smooth.

"They sure grow the miles long in North Carolina," Royce retorts.

When the Beechcraft touches the runway, Dan finishes his left turn onto final approach, less than one mile from the runway, and lines up for the landing. Dan would love to make a nice three-point landing on his first flight. Instead, he touches down a little forward and crooked, and the plane begins pulling to the right, in a "crab" response. Dan corrects the swerve, and the plane takes a straight path down the runway.

> *"In the air, decisions don't wait a long time. You can't pull over and stop."*

He knew the landing would be tough, because of the distinctive configuration of the landing gear. In contrast, the typical tricycle gear, with one wheel forward and two back, places the center of gravity in front of the main wheels. Because of this, whenever the plane begins to swerve, "it wants to straighten out, because the center of friction pulling on the wheels is behind the center of gravity," Dan explains. "The center of gravity wants to keep it straight. It's almost self correcting." But the 185 won't help the pilot during a landing. The center of friction lies in front of the center of gravity.

If the 185 touches down slightly crooked, the center of gravity wants to swing the tail to the side in an effort "to swap positions with the center of friction," Dan says. If the rear does swing forward, the wheels will begin to chirp. That did not happen on Dan's landing. If it had, however, and it was not quickly corrected, the wing tip could have struck the surface in what is known as a "ground loop." The ground loop can have other negative consequences. "You may break off the landing gear," Dan says, "and the propeller may hit the ground as well. If it does, you ruin the engine!"

Once back at Moody Aviation, Dan completes the post-landing procedures and refueling. Later, after he has helped guide the plane back to the hangar, Dan thinks about his first flight in the Skywagon. He declares the flight "fun," more fun than he expected, and he calls the plane a pleasant surprise. "It's a challenge that makes me want to do it right. There's a lot I must do—a lot more piloting—with the tail on the ground. It's work, but I like it."

On the mission field, the Cessna 206 is gaining popularity because of its greater utility. But scores of 185s fly the mission skies, so Dan appreciates the lessons he has to take. It requires an alert pilot, one whose skills can make a ride comfortable and safe for passengers. Skills and alertness are crucial when flying in remote regions of the world, so Dan knows the importance of these lessons.

He will go aloft in the Skywagon many more times this year, on his way to amassing more than 350 flight hours. Soon he will begin a series of "check rides" to refine his skills. Like his journeys in the 172, Dan will take the 185 skyward to encounter unusual situations that will measure and mature his flight judgment. His flight instructor will put him in imaginary and sometimes actual settings where Dan must make quick decisions.

The check flights allow the instructor to observe the student's judgment. "We can observe what he can do and his decision making. If there are weaknesses in his performance, we can talk about it," says chief flight instructor Bill Powell.

Check flights are one part of being sure Moody graduates possess both the skills and wisdom needed for missionary flying. Sometimes a student with great flying and mechanical skills is weak in decision making. "He may be coordinated and make the plane do what he wants," Powell says. "But he's vulnerable in tense situations where he must make a decision. Unfortunately, in the air, decisions don't wait a long time. You can't pull over and stop." Dan looks forward to future flights in the Skywagon, including check flights. With the 185, Dan notes, "the pilot has to *make* the plane behave." But he adds that the pilot's increased involvement makes the job exciting, even fun. "It's work, but I like it."

13

Pilots, Male and Female

Dan Morgan is not the only third year student "fired up about missions and mission aviation," as he describes his zeal to be a missionary pilot. So are Tom Ferguson, John Munsell, and Dan Whitehead. Like all Moody Aviation students, they arrive with a strong commitment to aviation as ministry. Each year they renew that commitment by signing the school's statement of intent, declaring missionary aviation as their goal. It is a promise they make to their school, to themselves, and to God. Tom, John, and Dan typify the pilots Moody produces.

When Tom Ferguson finished his computer training at Samford University in Alabama, he became a computer programmer and earned a good salary. But having recommitted his life to serving Christ while a college senior, he soon felt limited in his chances to help people. He had become a Christian at age eight but, at times, had wandered until his recommitment in college. Now employed and drawing a good salary, Tom was not satisfied. "I asked myself, 'What can I do for people?' I looked at missions. When I told my wife, Jennifer, she got excited. She had been praying about missions. She set up meetings with mission agencies."

While living in Detroit, the couple listened as their pastor mentioned that nearby William Tyndale College offered flight training. At the local airfield where Tyndale students trained, Tom learned about Mission Aviation Fellowship, Jungle Aviation and Rescue Service, and other agencies. MAF and JAARS recommended a few schools, and after considering LeTourneau College and Moody Aviation, Tom applied to Moody Aviation, and his interest in mission service grew.

Unlike Tom, John Munsell always seemed a likely candidate for missions. His grandparents were missionaries with Central America Mission (now CAM International), and his parents often hosted visiting missionaries. "I always knew missions. I was saved at an earlier age, and in junior high I began a long look at missions. In high school I really committed myself to missions." As a high school senior he became aware of missionary aviation, and his older sister, a student at Moody Bible Institute, told him about the MBI flight program.

Tom's interest in missionary aviation links two loves—missions and mechanics. "I've always been interested in mechanical things and working with my hands. I think I have the gift of service. I enjoy helping people in practical ways. As a result, aviation seemed like the perfect way to serve."

John admits that sometimes he gets excited about "the technical things I'm learning," and he must remember his purpose is training to serve people. "As I prepare to go overseas, I want my focus to be ministry to people over there. I must keep my eyes open for ministry." He now helps direct high school and college activities at a church in Johnson City, a few miles from Elizabethton. After graduation he plans to serve as a short-term missionary with Flying Mission in Botswana, Africa. Afterward he will return for a year of flight and maintenance work before becoming a missionary pilot, either with Flying Mission or another agency.

Like John, Tom faces distractions from ministry and spiritual growth while a flight student. During his second year, he fell behind in his studies and felt the pressure of a heavy course load. His wife and his relationship with God brought balance back. Occasionally, Jennifer and Tom would take a weekend getaway, both to relax and to remember that they came to Elizabethton to prepare for ministry. "That's how I cope with stress, by getting away." His spiritual life also helps him gain perspective, though an unusual temptation faces many Moody pilots in town, according to Tom.

"Being here, I thought spiritual growth would automatically come. [But] people in town brand you as a 'Moody' and tend to put you on a pedestal. It's easy to develop spiritual pride and let everything relax.

"It takes a lot of effort to remember what's important. I need to humble myself and stay in the Word. It's easy to say, 'Well, we have chapels here every day. Why do we need anything else?' I'm trying to learn consistency. I still struggle with that."

Tom and Dan both have learned the art of saving money for their flight training. Becoming a missionary pilot is not an inexpensive proposition. For their flight time, insurance, tools, and books, students will spend more than $25,000 during their three years. Though Moody Bible Institute provides a three-year subsidy for each student,[1] students often apply for financial assistance through student aid. To be eligible for the grant, a student must show need, demonstrate good potential for success, and meet academic criteria.[2] In addition, students may qualify for a Moody student loan, an interest-free loan of up to $6,000 per student, available in the student's junior and senior years.

Before enrolling at Moody Aviation, John had saved money by working during summer breaks while an undergraduate student at MBI and then working full-time after graduation for a year. Cash gifts from his parents and earlier savings also helped him pay for first-year expenses in his airframe and powerplant courses. To pay bills his final two years, funding comes from several sources: his parents give money, several Christian friends support John, and he has received two school loans.

Tom came with $15,000 from his savings, and Jennifer's salary as a nurse helps. But during the final two years, aid from friends in Chicago has declined, and the rates have increased drastically. He estimates his cost for the three-year program, including insurance, projects, and extracurricular activities, "is pushing $30,000." Tom also has benefited from a $6,000 MBI loan, but as Jennifer expects their first child and prepares to leave her job, they know the loss of her income and new family expenses await. They will meet with their pastor soon to see if their church will consider supporting them as prospective missionaries.

Flight costs are rising, Director Simmelink notes, and students learn the principles of missionary support early. "We encourage them to develop a correspondence base because our graduates someday will be with a mission where they will probably generate a support base. 'Tell these people what you are doing and your goals,' we say. Some students have churches that already help them in their training, anticipating the time when they will be missionaries from their churches. God provides in so many ways. In spite of the high costs, I do not know of any student who has had to drop out of training here for financial reasons."

Dan Whitehead, another third year student, wonders more about his age than about his finances. At thirty-two, he is among the older students in a program that prepares pilots for long-term mission service. "Whenever I meet with a mission board, my first question is, 'Am I too old?' So far, many have been encouraging." Dan has met with representatives of JAARS and MAF. He wants to serve in Latin America, though he realizes the two agencies appoint pilots to areas of current need, so his choice may not be honored. South America Mission appeals to Dan, but at present they have no needs for additional pilots. With applications at all three organizations, he continues to explore possibilities and pray.

"Once he finishes his candidacy and we turn him loose, he's a pilot in command. He's basically running an airline on the other side of the world."

Dan has a great background for cross-cultural ministry. He has visited thirty-seven countries in five years as a member and then as conductor of The Continental Singers, a Christian touring group. He also has an academic minor in Spanish. He helped The Continentals start a ministry in Latin America by assembling Latino teens (Puerto Rican, Mexican, and Venezuelan) in Puerto Rico who then toured Central and South America. The experience increased his appetite for missions.

His cravings first came during his initial tour with the group through the daily Bible studies and prayer times with Continental members. A recent graduate of a small liberal arts school in Pella, Iowa, he had finished four years of voice and had a degree in music, only to become a retail manager in a sporting goods store. *Why did I spend $25,000 to get a music education, and here I am doing this?* Dan wondered. So he joined the Continental Singers to sing and travel.

"At the time, I was thinking more about music than getting close to other Christians," he admits. "Music turned out to be one-eighth of what the group was about." During their rehearsal camp and continuing during the tour, Dan found himself thrown into thorough discipleship training. The program, he reflects, "helped me to develop some maturity in the Christian life." The final discipleship lesson focused on "developing a Christian worldview," Dan says. Combined with his travels through Europe and the Americas, the studies made him take a strong look at cross-cultural missions. Now, like all the students at Moody Aviation, Dan Whitehead has responded to God's call to missions by training to become a missionary pilot.

After graduation, most of these pilots will work at least one year before serving overseas. Nothing beats hands-on experience in a shop or in the air. Most JAARS pilots have at least three years experience Stateside,[3] and MAF encourages pilots fresh from flight school to work at least one year in general or commercial aviation as pilots or mechanics before joining them.

"We are more concerned about the maturity of an individual than his technical ratings," says Ken Frizzell, MAF chief operating officer. He says maturity cannot occur in "a controlled school environment." The graduates of Moody and other flight schools must make a transition from being a student to being a peer. "We look toward seasoning the airman and creating a mature pilot in the field. He has to become a problem-solver. Once he finishes his candidacy and we turn him loose, he's a pilot in command. He's basically running an airline on the other side of the world."

Most new pilots are glad to wait before joining a mission agency. Often graduates have student loans to repay, and a job lets the recent grad clear debts and reestablish a savings account. For older students with strong training from schools such as Moody, MAF will accept them to full candidate status, according to John Fairweather, manager of technical resources at MAF. "They're green and they know it. But they have a good, firm foundation to build on. We can work with that."

Aviation experts agree that today's missionary pilot differs from aviators a generation ago. Though new pilots are making longer commitments to missions, Fairweather says the era of lifetime commitments to aviation ministry is probably over. "In the early nineties, we are getting people who are looking more to [the] long-term [needs of their families]. I don't think they are looking to thirty-five years with MAF. But that's OK. We would love to see them involved with MAF for fifteen to twenty years."

Why no longer than twenty years? Fairweather says most men will consider career changes by their mid-forties, while they still have their productive years. "From the time our staff comes in, we talk with them about planning their career. We recognize that their career with MAF may start today but may not continue [beyond fifteen years]. Not everybody is content to fly a 185 or 206 all their lives. It can be hard work, loading and unloading cargo, dealing with weather problems. We recognize that the Lord is able to lead people into a ministry organization, and He is able and does lead people out of one ministry into another."

Fairweather himself has been in MAF for twenty-eight years. He admits that he pondered leaving MAF when he was forty-four. "Most of our men by age forty-two answer that question of change."

Frizzell says a pilot's shorter commitment period "models to some degree the current trends and lifestyle that is part of the U.S. and Canadian church. In the work environment adults spend about three years in one job. Our current tenure among pilots is 10.6 years."

In addition, today's pilots are keenly aware of their families' needs, Frizzell notes. Through the early seventies, the pilots considered themselves specialists and problem solvers. "Give them a bobby pin and a piece of lint, and they would make a Betamax. They were resourceful people who found a way to get the job done. They were resilient to hard times and tough conditions. They prided themselves on a make-do, macho image.

Barkman believes a pilot's values shift during the first term and that the pilot becomes aware of the change when he returns to the United States.

"We've worked hard to leave the macho image [behind], because it created . . . an image of a bush pilot, a Christian version of a swaggering, scarf-around-the-neck, goggles-type pilot who delivered the mail. Of course, the accidents followed. We've tried to move our pilots to a much more professional devotion to their task. In doing that, we have become a relatively benign airline, and pilot-candidates can become more interested in the side benefits than in taking pride in the job itself, which God has given them to do." Not all candidates are that way, but more are interested in provisions for their families rather than the type of plane they have. "They're worried about their retirement, their dental care, their work hours."

Missions itself is changing, Frizzell notes, and so MAF is looking for a different kind of pilot than previously. Missions is ministry, not an enterprise, and sometimes pilots need to be reminded of what makes up ministry. Ministry occurs "when I vicariously have a work by serving a missionary," Frizzell says. "The pilots must see that in serving they are ministers, they are fulfilling God's call on their life. Ministry is any activity that moves someone closer to Christ. That may be medical or lifestyle evangelism. As a believer, I have a role—a privilege—to encourage, to invite, or to somehow move you closer to the centrality of Christ in your life.

"Our pilots can encourage a person to move toward Christ in a lot of ways. Whether they're flying a missionary, an atheist, or an Islamic merchant, we want our pilots to show Christ in their lives."

JAARS Executive Director Eldon "Butch" Barkman says that pilots tend to make short-term commitments and are more interested in side benefits and in details about the organization itself. "But give these new people a term on the field, and they're wonderful!" he exclaims. "When they return a second term, they have a drastic change in attitude toward service."

Barkman believes a pilot's values shift during the first term and that the pilot becomes aware of the change when he returns to the United States. Back home, "they're viewing the values their friends have and looking at their own values—values they have learned in the first term of service. They ask themselves, 'Have I changed, or have they changed?' They finally conclude, 'Well, I have changed!'"

Barkman tells his veteran missionaries watching the first-timer, "Be patient, they will come around. They just have further to go than you did twenty years ago." The rookie pilots absorb the new values through experiences with nationals and by observing and talking with other American missionaries working in the area, according to Barkman.

One trait among mission pilots has not changed over the years: their gender. Pilots remain overwhelmingly male. The reason is neither agency discrimination nor lack of interest among women. Instead, the male-dominated cultures of the Third World countries where most missionary pilots fly regard women as inferior and hesitate to deal with them as peers. Women missionaries receive no cooperation from male leaders, especially in Islamic cultures.

Betty Greene shaved almost ten days off a Peruvian river trip by flying a plane across the Andes at 18,500 feet.

Many women who consider aviation leave before they reach the field, says MAF's Frizzell. He cites three reasons: the patriarchal society that refuses to deal with women; the heavy physical work of unloading cargo, often alone; and the shift to using nationals as pilots. At MAF, women participate as mechanics and flight followers, and serve in the home office. "But in the line operations, where we operate the tanks in the field, we look at a unique situation," Frizzell says.

Betty Greene was one of mission aviations's first pilots, but few women have followed her. As MAF's first overseas pilot, Betty flew in Peru, parts of the Sudan, and Irian Jaya (then Dutch New Guinea). In 1946 she shaved almost ten days off a Peruvian river trip by flying a plane across the Andes at 18,500 feet. Wearing an oxygen mask as she flew a single-engine Grumman Duck from one river to another, she could fly cargo between an island base and a mission outpost in one and one-half hours, compared to ten days by boat.[4] Yet even Betty Greene, a missionary aviation pioneer, had her limits. She needed help to load and unload equipment and supplies, Frizzell says.

"It's a young man's job, and it's heavy, physical work. It's demanding work. Most women have strengths, but they lie in other areas than upper-body strength," Frizzell adds. Pilots load a diverse cargo today, from live cattle to fifty-five gallon drums of gasoline. A full drum of kerosene can weigh almost four hundred pounds. Frizzell remembers one MAF pilot who in one day loaded and unloaded lumber totaling fifteen tons. "He had thirty shuttles that day—one thousand pounds in the plane, one thousand pounds out."

"The door has been open. We encourage women," says JAARS Executive Director Barkman. He believes some women are physically capable of the hard labor. But the Third World culture limits their effectiveness. "A woman in the bush is among women who have no rights. Those things concern us. They can be abused in various ways. They would not be respected, because they are not a man."

Moody Aviation has had one woman complete her flight school training. Debbie Schrenk Pinardi was graduated in 1989 but did not enter missionary service, marrying and becoming a mother a couple years later. In the past six years, two women have served as missionary pilots. At MAF, Canadian Gina Jordan has acted as copilot in a large Cessna twin-engine plane flying in Zaire. Formerly with MAF-US, she is now with MAF-Canada and copilots a twin-engine plane in Kenya. When time comes to unload supplies, she joins her copilot and the local staff to move the cargo.

Frizzell believes there will also be room for women in "unique situations." However, in the small single-engine planes, "the strip by strip, itinerant work does not lend itself well to a woman. In these cultures she would not gain respect. She could not act as pilot in command and expect to get the male general into the back seat when he wanted

179

to be up front. The dynamics of these cultures don't follow the sensitivities here in the West."

In Peru, Pierre and Phoebe Lagenouse served as a husband and wife team for Wings of Hope-Canada (*Avion Sans Frontiers*). Phoebe flew the plane, and Pierre maintained it. The Canadians served missions along the Amazon River. "She flew the airplane until she was seven months pregnant," recalls Barkman, who knows the Lagenouses from his time flying in Peru. "The people would load and unload the aircraft, and she would make sure it was tied down properly. She would crank up her float plane, they would push her off, and she'd be gone." After their first child, the Lagenouses returned as a family to serve a few years in Zaire.

The Betty Greenes, Gina Jordans, and Phoebe Lagenouses are all part of the heritage of missionary aviation. Hoping to join them soon are young pilots like Tom Ferguson, John Munsell, and Dan Whitehead. Tom, John, and Dan will be part of a worldwide force of pilots active at more than forty missions—most small but all vital enterprises. In the next chapter we will meet the pilots and leaders of these smaller missions and look at the future of mission aviation.

Notes

1. In 1990 the subsidy was $9,700. Figures come from an interview with Ken Simmelink, Moody Aviation director, on November 28, 1990.
2. Interested readers can send donations to Moody Aviation Student Aid Fund, Stewardship, Moody Bible Institute, Chicago, IL 60610.
3. Interview with Paul Duffy, MAF assistant to the president, April 22, 1991.
4. Lee Roddy, *On Wings of Love* (Nashville: Thomas Nelson, 1981), pp. 16-20.

14

From the Amazon to Zaire

The thick, lush vegetation of the Amazon rain forests is both inviting and forbidding. Missionaries may admire the exotic butterflies and brilliant toucans and macaws, but they also will face mosquitoes and fist-sized beetles. On the mighty Amazon River that stretches two thousand miles across northern Brazil, they may eye alligators and water snakes just beyond their dugout canoes. That's one reason they appreciate the planes of the Association of Baptists for World Evangelism (ABWE), Baptist Mid Missions, Gospel Missionary Union, and New Tribes Mission. But the missionary pilot also brings welcomed supplies and medical care in hours, making the missionary's life safer and his ministry more efficient.

In Benjamin Constant, Brazil, one thousand miles from the nearest large city and close to the Colombia and Peru borders, Clif Jensen has been flying seaplanes for ABWE since 1981. He shuttles missionaries, nationals, and supplies between stations and Benjamin Constant, and often flies passengers to Amazon Baptist Hospital for emergency medical assistance. Operated by ABWE, the hospital is located 175 miles down the Amazon from Benjamin Constant. The trip that required twenty long, tiring hours by boat is just one and one-half hours by floatplane. (A return boat trip would take thirty hours against the river's current.)

Clif does much more than ferry passengers from point to point, however. "At ABWE, you're a missionary first and a pilot second," he says. ABWE pilots typically are active in evangelism and church planting like other ABWE missionaries. The pilots preach regularly in established congregations, offer follow-up Bible studies to believers, and train church leaders for teaching and preparing lessons.

The pilots are on the ground frequently since they fly for a small aviation ministry—ABWE has 13 active pilots and eleven planes—unlike MAF, where more than 110 pilots serve many missions. The ABWE pilot must carefully divide his time between these teaching and preaching ministries and the transportation needs of missionaries and others. Passengers include pastors of established Brazilian churches reaching out in evangelism to other areas. They help ABWE meet a key goal—having national churches produce other national churches.

Clif is a graduate of Cedarville (Ohio) College, a Christian liberal arts school, and Moody Aviation. Although he lacks seminary training, his strong Bible background has been a welcomed addition at a local church. Clif has served as pastor there for several years, after the national pastor left the area.

"A love for the people, a deep concern for the welfare of their souls, and some basic teaching skills are what one needs," Clif says. "The real challenge has been to present biblical truth at the intellectual level of the listener. This has forced me to teach the Bible not necessarily as I have been taught, but in a way these river-dwellers can see the truth [in] their own social and cultural settings.

Many of the forty mission agencies have less than a dozen pilots, and flights are limited to one continent.

ABWE tries to have two pilots for each plane, each active in ministry. Pilots divide their duties according to their interests, abilities, and schedules. "By sharing the load and responsibilities, the pilots perform more effectively, reducing both stress and fatigue," Clif adds. The tandem flying approach also helps during furloughs. When one pilot is on furlough, the other continues the work uninterrupted; the second is already familiar with the people and the terrain, and neither time nor expertise is lost.

Most mission aviation agencies, like ABWE-AIR, are much smaller than MAF and JAARS. And like ABWE-AIR, they all have distinct policies and philosophies of ministry. Many of the forty mission agencies have less than a dozen pilots, and flights are limited to one continent; some serve only one mission, some only one country. Missionary Aviation Repair Center, Arctic Missions, and Alaska Village Missions fly aircraft only in Alaska. And as their name implies, pilots for SAM-Air serve missionaries with South America Mission.

SIMAIR, based in Niger, has only three pilot/mechanics and one mechanic. They fly in three west African countries—Niger, Benin, and Burkina Faso—serving SIM International missionaries and the local villagers, often bringing foodstuffs and medical aid. "Our main goal is moving people—missionaries between stations and church leaders to conferences," explains Jim Rendel, a SIMAIR pilot for almost twenty years.

Rendel, a Moody Aviation graduate, was the first SIMAIR pilot to be placed in Niamey, the capital of Niger and main base for all its flights. "Niger is eight hundred miles across and 75 percent desert, so travel is difficult and the distances great. SIMAIR is an integral part of SIM [created] to help in any way it can with the overall goal of evangelism and church planting."

ABWE's aviation ministry is similar to SIMAIR in that it usually flies in support of a parent mission. ABWE, an association for independent Baptists, has missionaries in twenty-one countries. Compared with SIMAIR, ABWE-AIR is a medium-size aviation mission. Its thirteen pilots are active in five countries: Brazil, Paraguay, Peru, the Philippine Islands, and Togo. An aviation program in Colombia closed recently due to threats from guerrillas and drug traffickers.

These smaller agencies are just as important as MAF and JAARS, which dominate mission aviation—so important that the two larger organizations often will lend personnel and expertise to the smaller missions when requested. Both have assisted SIMAIR, for instance.

MAF increasingly is serving national churches in Third World countries and using national workers to staff airports.

MAF, the first mission aviation agency, has eighty-seven aircraft, ranging from Cessna single-engine planes to the fast Beechcraft twin-engine turboprop, and operates in nineteen countries.[1] They serve most evangelical mission agencies by ferrying missionaries, national pastors, and lay leaders, moving ill villagers to hospitals in medical emergencies, and supplying missionaries with food and equipment. JAARS has thirty-one planes and two helicopters, flying overseas in eight countries.[2]

As missions has changed, so has missionary aviation. Increasingly pilots are flying national pastors because, as missionaries train the nationals to replace them as pastors and evangelists, their numbers are growing. Veteran pilot John Fairweather says Mission Aviation Fellowship was "solely a servant of missions" during its first twenty-five years. By 1973, however, developing national churches were changing MAF's mission. "They were beginning to stand on their own two feet. Whether they wanted or needed the airplane, they took charge of evangelistic outreach in their area," says Fairweather, now MAF technical resources manager with twenty-eight years of MAF service. "By the mid-seventies, we were not only a servant of missions, but we were also there to serve the national church."

"Years ago we entered Zaire, Irian Jaya, Brazil, and Mexico at the request of a North American mission." In contrast, a national church already existed in West Kalimantan, Indonesia, when MAF entered in the mid-eighties, according to Fairweather. Now MAF increasingly is serving national churches in Third World countries and using national workers to staff airports.

MAF President Max Meyers recalled some of the dramatic changes of the past forty-five years of missionary aviation in a special anniversary issue of the MAF magazine, *LifeLink.*

"When I was flying with MAF in the 60s, 80 percent of my passengers were white missionaries. Today, the majority are nationals. . . . Early on, we were often seen as part of a white colonial structure. Now we must stand in long lines waiting for visas from Third World nations. . . .

"In some places the needs are greater today than they were in 1945. In Zaire, for instance, there were twice as many miles of usable road in the 1940s than now, so . . . aviation support is even more important. . . . Aviation technology has also changed. In the early days, pilots used 'dead reckoning' navigation to cross the jungle. In some areas today we use electronic systems that can pinpoint our flight position within 100 yards."[3]

Missionary fliers will remain indispensable in the 1990s and beyond because their skills are indispensable, according to aviation officials. JAARS Executive Director Eldon Barkman calls Africa "the challenge of the future." He predicts that the growing Christian church will welcome missionary linguists to translate the Scriptures into local languages. Those linguists will need missionary pilots to fly them there.

Bob Gordon, a former pilot/mechanic in Haiti and Zaire who has served thirty years with MAF, says the pilot's call to show God's mercy will remain an attractive—and essential—way to present the gospel. During his flights in Zaire he flew in educational, agricultural, and medical help, and, of course, food. He once flew fertilized eggs raised by a local church into remote villages where disease had destroyed most of the chickens. "That church helped the people to get started with the chickens. This brought protein into their villages" and assured the people's health. "When you do those types of things, people listen to what you have to say about other things. It's a platform that leads to evangelism."

That's why the missionary pilot will always be a missionary. "Yes, the pilot supports missionaries, but he also is a missionary," emphasizes Moody Aviation's Bill Powell. As a pilot in the Philippines, Powell demonstrated his faith to the Filipinos who lived with him. Two house girls helped the Powells as they hosted guests in Bagabag and raised a son and daughter. Now fully grown, the women both serve with Wycliffe Bible Translators. One translates the Scriptures; the other is in nursing. Their times with the Powells led them to a Christian commitment.

In some countries a trend to restrict visas continues, and the pilot's work becomes more crucial. He and other missionaries are planting churches that one day may endure alone, if governments ban the missionary presence. Even now some countries only allow pilots to come in to train nationals to fly and repair planes. Those pilots are gaining the respect of nationals and a platform to present the gospel as they work. The pilots are "tentmakers" like the apostle Paul, using their profession to gain entry into people's lives. They have evangelistic opportunities they lacked decades ago.

"Our responsibility is to harness aviation to the needs of the mission field."

However, other pilots and missionaries soon may be denied visas to minister in certain countries, and they see the 1990s as a golden time to establish God's church while they can. Powell explains the power of training nationals to take over by looking at his now-grown, now-Christian house girls. "If Wycliffe pulls out of the Philippines, the women are there as part of a Filipino translation team." Other Filipinos who accepted Christ as their Savior by observing the love of the Powells also could continue a Christian witness. "Living our lives before them, from a Christian standpoint, and becoming friends, we saw several come to the Lord.

"The airplane is the excuse for being there, but being there is a ministry itself. I was able to reach people, as were several other missionaries," Powell notes. And it's a minis-

187

try that can continue in lives if the missionary one day must leave.

Meanwhile, mission pilots remain indispensable in many countries, winging missionaries to remote places where they either cannot travel or do so at great personal risk. In Zaire, for instance, roads have seemingly disappeared, declining from 60,000 miles of roadway in 1960 to less than 7,500 miles in 1990.[4] On those 7,500 miles of roads, Fairweather notes, "you can drive a pickup, but you can't use a car."

From Nate Saint to Clif Jensen, the missionary pilot continues to be part of God's plan to complete His kingdom, men who fly the gospel to remote regions of the earth. From the Amazon to Zaire, they are God's fliers. Their spiritual mandate will not change. "Our pilots want to further the gospel and help people," Fairweather declares.

In a letter sent to his friends just before his departure to Ecuador, Nate Saint described his mission as an MAF pilot. "In Ecuador we'll fly . . . down the [Andes'] eastern slope to the foothills and the little Shell Oil camp located where the road yields to jungles and missionaries to mules. Beyond lies the vast dungeon of the mighty Amazon where thousands are bound in darkness by the chains of sin. . . . We are not expecting the airplane to usher in a workless golden age for the missionaries but rather it will be used as a tool that will let them push ahead more effectively.

"We say that God could use even menial things like airplanes if they were dedicated to the reaching of the lost. Our responsibility is to harness aviation to the needs of the mission field."[5]

Almost a half century after Saint's words, that welcomed harness continues to lift missionary aviators skyward in service to missions and to the Creator of the heavens.

Notes

1. Data for 1989 in brochure "Carrying the Torch For the Lord," MAF, Redlands, California, May 1989.
2. Data for 1991 from Office of the Executive Director, JAARS, Waxhaw, North Carolina, May 1991.
3. Max Meyers, "Flight Plan," *LifeLink* (Winter-Spring 1990), p. 2.
4. Interview with John Fairweather, MAF, Redlands, California, February 15, 1991.
5. Russell T. Hitt, *Jungle Pilot: The Life and Witness of Nate Saint* (New York: Harper & Brothers, 1959), p. 142.